M000306939

LIVE
FREE

Your Journey to a Liberated Life

LIVE
FREE

Your Journey to a Liberated Life

The Kinepathics Approach to
Physical, Emotional and Sexual Wholeness

ANITA DE FRANCESCO, M.A.

LIVE FREE: *Your Journey to a Liberated Life*
The Kinepathics® Approach to Physical, Emotional and Sexual Wholeness

Copyright© 2008 Anita DeFrancesco
www.kinepathics.com
anita@kinepathics.com
www.tantrawisdom.com
info@tantrawisdom.com

310.210.1464

Rosey Publishing
PO Box 2431
Philadelphia, PA 19147

Printed in the United States of America

PROJECT CREDITS

Cover design:	Stephanie Yuhas - www.Shinygrape.com
Design:	Peter Zales - www.affordableoffset.com
Editing:	Lisa Wells - www.authorlhyoung.com
Printing:	Keystone Digital Press - www.kdpress.com

LIBRARY OF CONGRESS CATALOGING-IN PUBLICATION DATA
ISBN-13   978-0-9822616-0-6
ISBN-10   0-9822616-0-8

Contents

Dedication

This book is dedicated to all those people who have ridiculed me, bullied me, raped me, hurt me, loved me, nourished me, put me down and so on, because if it wasn't for you I would of never learned.
I thank you all and inspire you to turn your life around.

For my mother Rose, who suffered for love.

Acknowledgements

Acknowledgements go out to the God in all of us and my two favorite nieces Janelle Pearce and Lauren Pearce. Thanks to my sister Andrea Ilisco, and my great nephew Nicholas Lanza. Thanks to Coralee Zaremba for her friendship; Prema Deodhar for her belief and admiration; Mike Carlin of *Century City News* for being supportive with my "love buzz" column; Carl Alberici, Andrea Garfield and Marianne Karou for her enlightenment; Arun Lata Sharma, Lisa Leotta for her song *Miracles*, Christian Yates; authors Marianne Williamson and Sondra Ray for inspiration; Craig Johnson for his wonderful word; Tim Shullberg for his stalwart support; Saraswati (Sara Brown); Wesley Wolcott for his love and generosity; Sandra Caruso for her belief in me; Auggie Luna for his love and support; Albena Teofilova for her admiration; Andy Hartnett for his freedom (free me); Regina Poolos for being a cool cousin; Larry (Lucky) Otting for his open heart; Francesca Jacobs for her soul in the moment; Joe Vitale for his kindness, Barnaby Ruhe, RJ, Frank Rotella, Ana Rodrigues for her love; Stephen Higgins; John Brand for his passion; Tony Ricucci for his free spirit; Neil, Tony Malozza for he can see all; Sherri Brinks for her experience; Ned Smith for his support; Ann Standish for her support; Bond Wright for her care, compassion and talents; Robert Zirguilis for his friendship; John Dougherty who believed in me; Francois Favre who believed in me and helped me to see that.

"Be who you are not who you want to be."– *Anita*

Introduction

Love is one of the most powerful emotions and should not be something we suffer for but rather something we are that makes us stronger. Open your heart to your feelings and make peace with the world. Find the purpose in your life and you will personify love. Define yourself by exploring your nature, actions and thoughts. It's unconditional hate/fear versus unconditional love. The love side of this equation is experienced as inner joy. My advice is to make love to all that you do, regardless of what it is, and you will see how easy it is to become the "real you."

You are given a choice whether to love or to hate. Hate stems from fear, once that is out of the way you can begin the journey. The emotion you choose will become the driving force in all that you do. It is the ego force versus being in your body. When you stop complaining and accept where you are in your journey, then love will surface and your spirit will reign forever. There will be no such thing as death; only life. Regardless of what you're doing and who you're doing it with; love each and every moment because that's really all you have.

A lack of love leads to suffering. We are all suffering in one way or another. If we think we are better than others, then we are suffering. When we hate, we suffer because we cannot experience the beauty of life.

People with addictions, such as alcohol or drugs, are intimidated by their emotions. They fear the rejection they know they will receive by allowing their feelings to show. It's a known fact that these people have not been accepted in life and, along the way, have become afraid to be themselves. We also suffer from the evils in the world that seep into the positive psyche, making us believe in hate. Hate is real only if you give it life. It's like a disease that turns us into zombies, stealing the life in our beautiful spirits. When you hate, there is no room for the spirit. Perhaps that's why people drink and do drugs—because they have lost their spirit. Yet, it is these people that have the depth of feeling we long for.

How far has America gone so that hate is a priority over emotional sanity? I am here to tell you that you can set yourself free from the victimization. When we live and go about our daily lives in "hate" and "fear," we are, most definitely, a victim. It's not the person we hate that is the victim, but you, the hater. So, for every time you do or say that you hate something or someone, you are the victim. Therefore, you are suffering. The controllers, violent people, haters, egotists, and so on, are all suffering. They suffer from an overabundance of negativity. The people who have a need to be right all the time, indicating a fear of abandonment or death are suffering. You need to wake up and notice this harmful mentality. *Take charge of yourself, pull yourself together, pick up and begin to truly live your life.* Suffering is part of letting go, you must be ready for the pain. Suffering with awareness leads to purification. I've accepted pain as purification.

The cells, or crucial building blocks, in our bodies suffer when we lack love. This can lead to disease. Love is the most powerful key to healing, freedom, and happiness. At what level of consciousness is love for you? It takes a spiritual journey and hard work in order to achieve the bigger picture. It is our life's destiny to find the place within us where love dwells.

I've learned to recreate the love that was hidden within me. It filled me with happiness and gave me purpose. You have to do the work, there is no other way. Stop complaining and make the effort to change. Stop hiding behind foolish behavior such as talking about other people, gossiping to pass conversation. It only develops false power. Remember that in the middle of tragedy there can be happiness. I took something from every experience in my life and put it together as a map of my journey as a collection of my experiences. Like all truths, I experienced the things in these pages personally, enabling me to write this book. At a very young age, I was encouraged by my own strength that gave me the direction of my journey through a process of subjective realization. When you begin your journey; you will experience passion like you never have before. This part of your life will make you feel so alive.

I learned about divinity by understanding the means with which I connected to others. I learned spirituality from life experiences so that organized religion was no longer necessary. Religion is a structured organization that is there to help people reach "the light of awareness". The strength of God became apparent in understanding my own life, my acceptance of truth. In actuality the only God that I know, is the one that lives within me. This is who I love and worship. With the realization of this spiritual side of my life, I became free from the ego in my mind. When we live too much in the mind we develop ignorance which is limited; I now open up to my deeper source of unlimited knowledge. I became free from the segregation of life. When we think with the ego we separate from other areas of our being. Then we wonder later why we complain.

Isn't it wonderful that we are here, experiencing this beautiful place called life? The trees, the flowers, the variety of weather, the people, the children, the pets, the material things, and this planet called Earth. Yes, life on land. I am so proud to be but one among so many different cultures, races, religions and I admire everyone for doing things in their own way. It's a privilege to be part of it. I want to thank you for giving me the opportunity to learn and care for my soul. If it weren't for the people who judged me, raped me, put me down, didn't hear me, stole my power, hated me, were jealous of me, loved me, helped me, nourished me, and ridiculed me, I would never have learned the ultimate with regard to my soul. Instead, I learned to experience the differences, to know that it's all of us, collectively, that make it happen—to be inclusive of the self and the planet, reaching for life in moments. I observed and took my inspiration from you. I encourage you to honor and celebrate your life, to find the moments in your day that purifies your heart. Just take a big breath in those wonderful moments.

This book is about how I came to be "in the present moment" from a serious childhood illness of the heart at the age of nine. As a result of suffering from rheumatic heart disease, I experienced an awakening from each and every experience along my life path. How? I surrendered and began to love myself. I became a great observer of the lives of others, watching and learning about people's experiences and accepting everyone for whom they were. The present moment "shifted" me and protected me. This book is about how I developed my inner world. How I built my inner foundation so that the outer world made sense and had direction. I understood my spiritual vision, allowing it to become my guide. My entire life has been spent looking straight ahead toward my life path without wavering. It's when we waiver that we are held back without direction. I challenge you to slow down, re-group and step into the new. Honor your life and take charge, because if you don't, who will? You have arrived. When you come to your own self realization, then you will understand letting go. Surrender to the new world and celebrate the now; remove the impurities from your thoughts and feel the magic.

People often ask me where I get my energy, stamina, Shakti, and presence for life. I simply tell them that I have built a reservoir of wisdom from the age of nine. I've learned to have a relationship with my feelings. For years I was judged and put down by many people, but I never let myself become a victim, because of the strong relationship I have with my feelings. Spiritually I wasn't being judged but rather mastered.

Other people say they want to have what I have, they want to be like me. But people pretend not to notice themselves. Others say that I am like them because we have had similar life experiences. It's important to find an identity of your own; "the real you." When I began to understand why I was here, I finally let go of the judgment and jealousy by choosing happiness. We become so attached to criticism that it becomes like a spinning wheel, causing us to feel off centered and confused.

I've learned over the years that if people cannot shoot you down with a gun, they will find another way to destroy you. They will be-little your sense of self and destroy your emotional well-being. It's really a big game to see who can stand up the longest in life. This happens in the corporate world where men and women fight for job advancements. Places in the public eye where racial and religious tensions spark wars. What is it all for? What are you trying to get away from, your ego? I find it tragically funny. Do people ever bother to take a look at what ails them, what drives them, for what their mission or purpose (dharma) is? Would you like to know what you should be doing? In order to answer this question, you have to open yourself enough to grasp the concept of learning in an atmosphere of together-ness. Instead of letting the negative things rule our thoughts, allow love to teach you more about yourself. This is what you're supposed to be doing. It is your contribution to life. Cleanse your karma and listen for the gentle, hidden voice of love to guide you. It's there—embrace it.

Along the way, there were many spiritual leaders that stepped into my path to enlighten and inspire me, bringing light into my life. I always recognized them when they appeared. They always found me. Spiritually, I was called to continue the path in more ways than one.

I had been working in Philadelphia (Philly) as an X-ray technologist and a public affairs reporter. I interviewed and took a class with relationships guru, Sondra Ray, author of *Loving Relationships*, who gave me a rebirth session in the 1990's. She encouraged me to move to California to continue my path. Later, I interviewed spiritual guru, Marianne Williamson in Philadelphia on a television station, where I had been working, about her book, *A Woman's Worth*. During the interview, I became inspired by her and related her life to mine. I came to the realization that it was the perfect time for me to go to California to continue my spiritual path. So I did.

Since Los Angeles is the cutting edge city for spiritual studies and leaders, it was necessary for me to join them. I studied Yoga, Psychology, Reichian and Bioenergetics Therapies, Tantra, Theatre, Dance movement and other spiritual studies. I came to continue my path, to get closer to my destiny. I founded the Kinepathics Approach of Life Solutions that are a series of exercises you will find at the back of this book.

The Kabbalah is a literary world of philosophy that we can learn a great deal from. Tantra Yoga is also a big philosophy of Hinduism and Buddhism with the power to transform us. What is it that you can teach today? Allow you to open and teach me. No matter how much you know, you still have so much to learn. Basically, we are ignorant to learning more about the self. Then we are in denial because we can never know enough—even if we hear it over and over. What we can grasp is "the truth." Stop saying "I know" and listen until you hear from your heart again and again. You do know!

Have you ever had the feeling that you were hurting from too much love, or from not enough? Have you ever had the feeling that you loved life so much that you couldn't wait to go to work that day? It was these two feelings that fed off each other day in and day out for me. Have you ever felt like you healed because of the pain and/or that love was just a destiny?

It has taken me half of my life to get my emotions where they need to be, to understand that, without these emotions in the right place, life is dull and ordinary. On a more positive note, I came to realize that the movement of my soul was not emotional, but rather an all-encompassing atmosphere of love—love that has its own destiny. I am writing this book in order to save the planet. That is, you and I working together with our own natures, striving for the betterment of all. This means teaching people to love themselves and others, one relationship at a time.

I grew up in Philly and a big part of the problem growing up in a city that was conservative therefore, not open to enlightenment was the repression. Philly was and still is suppressed mainly because of racial tension. People are afraid to interact with one another because of the way the political system there is run. Politicians don't care about people's feelings, therefore, they teach hate, thinking nothing of living with this mindset. If they "shifted" and became love, the potential for the city would be great—also, for the people. I have witnessed people drinking and doing drugs in all the inner cities like Philly and Detroit because they are governed by society so that they are afraid to experience their emotions.

Besides my own interest to share my story with you, I want you to know that this city that I grew up in is also known as the "city of brotherly love," yet it has the highest crime rate in the United States. I remember growing up with and between love and racial tension. Though I have been living in Los Angeles for fifteen years, I am still very connected to my roots in Philadelphia. No matter where we go, Philadelphians will never stop loving their native city. Why? It's because the word "love" is in the motto. In spite of its troubles, Philadelphia still retains the label of "Brotherly Love." I want to teach you what love really is—its' abilities to heal in the present moment. Love is a gift, it is formless, yet forms the essence of our being. Let's give and receive together. The more I suffer, the more I love. I use the suffering as a way to love, and open up to a deeper awareness. My spirit was trapped in my body until I discovered the unlimited source of knowledge.

In order to be empty of conflict, you must allow your mind to be free by pushing so that you are living on the edge of life instead of resisting it. Only then will you feel the fluid nature of liberation. It's a wave waiting to be harnessed by you—waiting to be ridden. No one should suffer. If you continue in a life of dishonesty, then you will always suffer. I give you hope, there is a way out, not around. Allow yourself a chance to go through life a little easier. Make a conscious decision to change. Let's breathe life into our dreams together. After years of perseverance, learning, and hard work, I give you Kinepathics.

"How can you lose when you can choose?"
-Craig Johnson

Anita DeFrancesco, M.A.
Los Angeles, California
Kinepathics
July, 2008

CHAPTER 1

My Journey to Kinepathics

A baby in the womb is a living being—waiting—but also is suspended in a regressive state of no return. It is very much like this strange state of life and death that kept me floating in my own presence. I made the choice, while in the womb, that I wanted life. To accept life is a choice. I chose to live. What will you choose?

"Life is a great place, if only you knew it existed!" - Anita

Before I begin my story, I want to share with you where it all began. There are certain philosophies that I believe you will find fascinating as well as a new way for you to look at things. I also want to share with you some of the experiences I've had as an adult that led me to these philosophies and, ultimately, to the creation of this book where I believe you can live out your life with profound meaning. We all take different journeys, but I believe that by teaching each other, our lives merge toward that powerful and consuming place called Love.

The way we live our lives on earth is a reflection of the way we were treated in the womb—whether we were loved or not, and whether we were wanted or not. Our society has long overlooked this major, silent contribution to understanding human behavior—this all important place of our roots, our beginning. The womb is a living vessel unto itself that requires nourishment and love in order to grow a life. The beautiful blossom harvested from the womb, is the child. If the parents mistreat the womb by negative thoughts and actions, an enemy is born within that precious baby. This is how the body is conditioned from generation to generation. That 'enemy' persona becomes a part of the newborn baby, later manifesting as false insecurities, negative attitudes, disasters, and illnesses. How do you want to pass on the Karma?

The fetus-in-growth is where human development begins; the womb sets the stage for the emerging child's performance, i.e. LIFE. From the moment of conception, the fetus is conditioned by the strong emotions and actions that filter through the womb to inadvertently affect our lives. This doesn't count any genetic preconditions. So, from the beginning it seems there are a lot of odds to overcome. This is why, when in the womb, all suffering begins.

My interest with the life we have in the womb is based on body movements and behavior. Emotions play a more powerful role in our lives than we realize. Emotional cleansing is just as necessary as brushing your teeth on a daily basis. Scientists believe that stress during pregnancy can cause the baby to have asymmetrical features that are revealed in the fingers or ears. In fact, a stressful pregnancy can affect the subsequent emotional, physical, spiritual, and mental well-being of a human life even before it takes that first breath.

Babies in the womb need as much love as they do after they are born. It is only recently that scientists have come to the belief that heart disease and high blood pressure actually begins in that place of stasis. Scientifically, that makes sense, but when you apply emotions and sensations, the big picture of our life becomes more understandable. The womb is our first environment. If you live in a dysfunctional environment, you take on the characteristics of that environment.

Scientists study genetic conditioning before birth as it relates to diseases. I'm investigating the behaviors, movements, and sensations that exist from life in the womb and then following the birth.

Because of the beautiful rituals, I think many of our religions and philosophies were trying to tell us something about this. The womb is sacred like the tabernacle, referred to as the "Body of Christ" in the Catholic faith. This is what the womb signifies; the richest, most powerful place in a woman's body. Patterns of self-expression begin and develop in the womb, just like the tiny arms and legs of the baby grow. The rhythm of life stems from our inner emotional behavior that also develops during our life in the womb. It is also in the womb that the emotional release of fulfillment begins to invigorate the expression of our soul. I have termed it the "Biologics of Behavior."

Womb Abandonment

Womb abandonment exists just as much as any abandonment we may experience in life. How do I know this so well? It was a first-hand, very graphic, experience that I'm sure many of you went through as well. Healing also begins in the womb. Ask your parents about your time in the womb. You might be surprised.

"Undulating my emotions." – Anita

I was in my early thirties when I actually recalled the experience when I attended a re-birthing session given by Sondra Ray, a relationships guru, whom I met in Philadelphia. Sondra Ray is the author of the book *Loving Relationships*, and is a re-birthing expert that finds the clarity of her energy in the constant repetition of being born time and again, much as I do in 'undulating my emotions.' When you are in the movement, you cannot hide. Re-birthing is a form of conscious, connected, deep breathing exercises. After many of these exercises, Ms. Ray asked me to tell her what I was experiencing. I responded by telling her that I felt, incredibly, as if I was a new infant traveling down the birth canal, but that I was surrounded by disease. The thickness of fluids blocked my breathing as I came into this world.

The birth canal is a space of incredible emotional trauma that should be reserved for the baby's freedom of movement. For every breath the fetus takes, more body space is needed in order to enhance its' spiritual security when the infant makes its' way into life. The way a woman cares for her womb, even when not pregnant, is a reflection of the future unborn. Young women need to cherish and praise the "yoni" space and protect it from abuse by self. Too many sexual partners take away from your freedom as an individual and deplete the positive spirit in your soul. No matter what kind of birth you experienced, the subconscious mind manifests the effects of the birthing process into our daily lives and our relationships with others.

"Birth was the first of my spiritual awakenings." – Anita

Sondra Ray believes that, when she was delivered, on a kitchen table, it made her subconsciously neurotic about food. Although most of her relationships with men were positive, she fell almost exclusively for restaurateurs.

In my own experience, I was born with disease all around my body on a Sunday. This experience has kept my body conscious, always looking to find ways out of the negative life. It was also special, bringing spiritual freedom since Sunday was always a day set aside for family, rest and religious services.

Re-birthing Therapies
"Trauma begins in the birth canal." – Anita

Rebirthing work, that includes breathing exercises, came from the experimental studies of Leonard Orr. He later co-wrote a book, *Rebirthing in the New Age*, with Sondra Ray . When Orr first experimented with these techniques, he noticed that he would often have what he described as "memories of his birth." Orr believed that by reliving his birth experiences through connected breathing, he was actually healing the trauma of his own birth. This discovery began in 1974 and has continued to develop.

The difference between Reichian orgone breathing and rebirth breathing is that with rebirth, you connect inhalation and exhalation from the mouth without pausing. In Reichian breathing, we breathe in through the mouth, take a slight pause, and then out through the mouth with a complete exhale of relief.

The birth of a baby is traumatic. This is due to ignorance and misunderstanding on the part of the medical professionals, parents and family. We never forget our birth; it's only a repressed memory. The way we are pulled from the womb is traumatic. The shining lights above us are also traumatic.

Our bodies have a cellular memory that is distributed from the brain cells throughout the body's tissues and organs. It is believed that trauma suffered during birth, and the specific nature of this trauma, has a deep effect on a person's psyche, thus shaping our perception and experiences of life, self and the world in ways we are mostly unaware.

Through rebirth therapy we are able to recall aspects of our birth and gestation period which helps to generate a positive shift. Rebirth therapy, Yoga, Kundalini and Reichian breathing all help to relieve suppression and provide greater insight into the human condition by helping us understand the purpose of our existence. It also gives us a greater sense of personal relevance to the world. The breathing exercises provide a direct physical experience of divine love through Pranic saturation of the body.

"Where does all the hate come from?" – Anita

Our emotions and spirituality are directly connected. Whether we acknowledge it or not, we all contribute to the hate in the world in one way or another. The more we let go of prejudice and judgment and see each other collectively as one and as the wonderful, individual people we are, the more love there is in all its forms. Once we begin to see everything as love and accept that love, the world will change little by little. It takes discipline and a willing courage of the heart. Now, clinging as we do, we are suffering from too much attachment. The difference between ordinary people and liberated living souls known as jivanmuktas, is that they eat and sleep like everyone else but they are not affected by what they do; there is no moisture of attachment. It is this liberation that gave me life.

"It's not about competing; it's about being." – Anita

Emotional Identity

Emotions are not a tangible substance we can hold in our hands, they're just sensations. We all have this emotional inner makeup that is a large part of our foundation. It needs to be exercised just like your physical body does.

Part of opening and being "real" is acceptance of vulnerability. A person's emotional identity is their emotional energy—it is fluid. It all begins with personality formation. Emotions are a delicate, sophisticated state to overcome. The mind finds its own rationalization to avoid emotions, but the heart would never understand. This is the reason many of us are living our own inner war. It's because we try to split ourselves into two halves, disconnecting from our whole being. When we learn to shift our emotional energy, this unrest will cease.

Part of connecting to your emotions is being honest. Honesty is organic. You can begin by being honest to the people around you, then to yourself. In order to experience your own feelings, you need to connect to one another. In society, children are permitted to express their emotions while, at the same time they are smothered. This stifling of human nature can lead to criminal behavior. Part of being the "real" you involves the external world. Part of opening and being "genuine" is vulnerability.

It's okay to adjust to your external situation and still remain who you are. You can be committed to anyone or activity and remain in your place—your identity. This is the focus of my Kinepathics teachings. I call it "identity strength."

Having an identity promotes the 'hidden wild personality'. This is the side of you desperately wanting to live. This inner wildness is the spirituality of your essence. It's simply who you are, thus "the real you." Celebrate, and experience your emotions, every one of them. By embracing your emotions, you grow and heal.

The first step in becoming comfortable with your emotions is acceptance. The range of human emotions is vast, spanning from happy, sad, fear, anger, love, and confusion, to name a few. In life we go through this spectrum of feelings, but at times we don't honor them. When we pull a muscle or tear a tendon, this can be an indication of not enough emotional attention, leaving us greedy for more. Kinepathics trains you to perform from the heart—from your whole being. An open heart leads to body expression. Emotional feelings and action behaviors all result in positive identity formation.

"You can still maintain your identity even when committed." – Anita

After opening your body, permission and freedom become one. I approach life from my deepest core so that I can experience the growth of my energy. When we know our identity, we can experience who we are, deeply and clearly. You know who you are, so admit it, be it, live it. You will begin to experience your higher power and your charisma will shine. Intuitively, you will feel your expressive nature emerge and know the direction and outcome of your decisions.

Your emotions are connected to every cell in your body—the 'real you,' the 'false you,' the 'hidden wild person.' Existing within our human-ness is a personality that we have yet to encounter. It's a whole other personality hidden, wanting to be released. When we use our creativity, we enable other elements within our dimension to live! People who rise above suppression and abuse have hidden personalities crying out to live. We, in our human-ness, find creative ways of hiding from our own hurts and from those who hurt us. People hide in many ways, such as through their voice, their movements, the way they dress, breathe and so on.

Referring to the womb, all the negativity and suppression sits in the pelvic floor. It's from this area that we move away from, that becomes the uncovered past; secrets hidden and the fears that threaten to overwhelm us. Emotions are behind everything we do. Emotions are the backbone of our structure. When our emotions have a basis in shock or go unexpressed, we are faced with stress. Emotions need to be contained so that they can be identified and defined. It is important to monitor your emotions and carefully contain them so that displaced anger does not affect others.

Once each emotion is identified, we can create separation, thus shifting the energy as well as the body and mind. We, as humans tend to layer new anger on top of old anger, creating a deep sense of conflict, thus loosing pleasant sensations. This is where vulnerability is crucial. Allowing yourself to feel your emotions is part of human nature. The amount of love you feel is the amount of love you are able to give to others.

We keep our emotions carefully cataloged and stored in a waiting area for us to let loose and live as we choose. Emotions are, also, a type of fuel; therefore, they must be stored and nourished within us. Emotions are energy. The amounts of stored emotions are your amount of potential energy, so it is crucial to embrace your emotions and be proud you have them. Tapping into our emotions gives us security, bringing equality to us all.

> *"The womb is a reconditioned self;*
> *the identity of the reconditioned self." – Anita*

Women are always giving birth in their lives to many things. We are naturally able to conceive the joy of the projects we take on. These projects become our 'babies,' so this is the way we function. Therefore, the womb gives women the opportunity to enhance our lives from the intrinsic core of the self. Whereby, men enhance themselves from the extrinsic core of the self. It's simple. It's the way we are made. *"Men's bodies project, (the penis), they can be measured, compared and assessed. Women's bodies invert. The vagina is amorphous, lurid in color, shapeless, impossible to quantify or architecturally simulate." – Camille Paglia.*

The beginning of my oppression had trickled down from societal attitudes so that it was experienced in the womb. For me, being born was a way of escaping my oppression. That's why we have the re-birth movement. Oppressive situations are pattern forming, and hard to escape. I struggled to stay alive in the womb, therefore, sometimes I find myself fighting to stay above the deep water in my life.

My life's purpose has become teaching the self-birthing experience to others through the art of Tantra. When I was born, I was able to connect to my physical self as if a sphere of motion. Through my parent's actions, I have learned that men look to women to give them birth to anchor them in life. This is simply the way things are. Women need to take charge of the family rather than controlling their mates and children. Controlling and taking charge are a big difference! Control is from the ego; a place with no emotion. Taking charge is an assertion of the mind and body to join with the emotions; thus, sharing.

In our time, women have moved from the pure feminine, combining with the masculine, (anima and animus), to survive the world of change, challenge and equality. Politics and the human equation are slowly coming together. The feminine and masculine, (yin and yang), essence exists in the people of today. This is part of integration. It is a direction that continually seeks and needs more harmony. I think men and women will eventually share the same sky.

"Miracles are nothing but the whirlwinds of emotion thrust - it is presence." – Anita

For me, even when I was celebrating my life, as I always do; I was born a miracle baby. In spite of my trauma in the womb, I broke through into this world on a Sunday morning, November 4th. It was a time of the baby boomers and President Eisenhower. I was a miracle baby in the womb just waiting my time for life. People often say that when good things happen, it's a miracle. It's actually presence.

Cultivating Presence

The more Shakti* energy we have, the more living in the presence we are. When we practice breathing along with clear, positive thinking, we teach ourselves to open up even more of who we really are. Intense breathing helps to develop positive cells thus optimistic thinking patterns. The more of our soul that we bare, the more 'presence' we reveal to others. Presence is happy energy that comes from nothingness. It is about positive change and learning. It has neither space nor time. It's the profoundness that we don't yet have an understanding of. This is a state of being into which we arrive. Presence is recognizing what doesn't belong to you while revealing who you are. Presence is a world of quiet shadows that functions from the natural processing of our consciousness.

When we have such an intimate connection to this source of energy, it helps us to confirm the choices we've made, and reveals our intimate purpose, as well as direction in life. Once we understand that we are responsible for our own direction, we simply find that we're at the beginning of our development. We create our own evolution—the progression of our own consciousness. When our consciousness stagnates from lack of beliefs, values or faith, we are blocking life's natural processes from developing. We all have presence, we just have to alter our reference of how, what and where we look for it. Emerging from the quiet shadow helps you to accept yourself and invites the clarity of your vision. By listening to the mind open and the way in which it develops, determines whether you remain caught within the momentary world or find newness within that world. If we recognize the transition as fleeting, without a permanence of its own, then one is said to be contradictory, or "between a rock and a hard place."

Truth is the way we express our trust without the attachment of fear. I am always honoring my presence—the present moment because of a suppressed life in the womb. As a result, I am able to cultivate that innate presence. It's the natural presence that allows and gives us the permission to float above the water.

"Every move is a celebration of life for me." – Anita

I started to believe in hope and became "the seeker." Every move I made in life, I cherished and so I became enlightened. This is what I am expressing to those of you reading this, that there is hope. In order to end your suffering, you begin by believing.

The stigma of oppression is within a person and once that person begins to open up toward another, then that person's life begins to open. This is what we need to understand in each other. Get rid of violent communication and understand the language of the heart. When we learn to communicate from our hearts, the ego dissolves and we become 'real.' This is the cultural way of Hinduism. (For further reading on nonviolent communication, see books by Marshall Rosenberg.)

"Love is stronger than death." – Anita

The Mother Earth

The energy of life revolves around the sexes. It's all about sex and these differences. Mother earth is in an era of suffering. We can see this clearly with the world crises and disastrous weather patterns. Global warming is inherently a part of mother earth. The feminine in all of us is suffering. The earth is the giver and sustainer of life. Gaia is the Greek goddess that personifies mother earth. The divine mother abides in the heart of every human that nourishes the Supreme Being; God the father. Mother earth is the giver of all birth and existence. Honor what's sacred and respect the fruits of the land. Have a greater appreciation for good and bad weather patterns, flowers, the soil, as well as the physical. When we appreciate life and love, the moments of life develop and give birth to the new earth.

*Shakti is often translated as the Goddess of Strength, meaning a sacred force, power or energy and is the Hindu concept of the divine feminine aspect that is sometimes referred to as the Divine Mother. For a more in-depth definition, see the glossary.

The Age of Chaos
"The movement of life is chaotic." – Anita

While in the womb, I experienced chaos which caused turmoil in my life, however, it helped me find my center. Chaos theory is the go-between that allows one to find a new direction that mediates between turbulence and coherence. The name "Chaos Theory" comes from the systems that are described by the theory as being disordered. What it's really about is finding the underlying order.

Chaos deals with unpredictable complex systems that stem in part from the work of Edward Lorenz, a graduate of MIT and meteorologist who simulated weather patterns on a computer. The term chaos tends to make a person think of crowds that are wildly out of control. However, in order to be in control, we need to be out of control. This is what chaos is. Though it may sound quite the opposite, chaos is actually a good thing. It's about releasing the inflexibility that we often project. In the womb, under such chaos, we have nowhere to go except to the center of our being to find order. With chaos, there is always a focus on confusion, but eventually, the external rhythm leads us back to the center. An example of this is when children spin around rapidly in circles and suddenly stop. They are solidly centered in a universe that appears to be whirling around them. Chaos creates regularity for me.

"Chaos is body maintenance." – Anita
Empathy begins in the womb. This is where we first begin our emo-

tional primal rhythms. My spiritual career began in the Uterus. I taught myself to shift from out of structure and pain, into life. From the before birth, I learned what life and death were all about. My spirit was strong and courageous. It was the spiritual relationship with the earth and the feminine for which I was born. It is from the nature of unbridled wildness that this spiritual relationship was born. It is the unknown that keeps us waiting. The mind must be prepared for the unexpected—the body must be conditioned to remain calm. In the middle of chaos there is freedom—much like the brief calm in the eye of a hurricane. Connect the unknown with the heart, then welcome and challenge it. Chaos, as it may seem, has a reason for existence, and the disorder that is chaos must eventually find its place among the limitations of order. Therefore, it can be surmised that chaos has a strength that dates back to the beginning of time.

"It's taking the mechanic out of the soul." – Anita

The Power of Gesture

Gesturing needs space, since it is when your thoughts become your actions. The 'present space' is always at your disposal. Gestures are your actions, your inner thoughts that take the place of words. (The strength of gesturing is alive and is very often part of our psychological behavior.) In human interaction, certain gestures can be as oppressive and hurtful toward others as any spoken negative words. If you've ever been the target of a pointed, accusing finger, you know how condescending it feels. Pointing with the hand or arm, on the other hand, can also be an extension of the body's inner strength, like when we lend a positive hand to someone who has fallen or bending toward someone in conversation, even pausing.

When we blow a kiss with a hand gesture; it's coming from a warm place inside indicating an affectation. Gesturing is an expressive part of nature like the branches of a tree that lean forward as if to embrace the child in us. People gesture to get a point across. It's like shaping and drawing your thoughts in the air. Gesturing is a wonderful tool when carefully acquired. It's dramatic articulation. Kinepathics trains you to create your own gestures from deep feelings and to articulate communication positively and effectively.

In Yoga we use the Sanskrit word "Mudras" to express gestures. Mudras manipulate prana in much the same way that energy, in the form of light or sound waves, is diverted by a mirror or cliff face. Mudras provide a means to access and influence the unconscious reflexes and the deeper primal instinctive habitual patterns.

"If men expressed their emotions; the womb is a person." – Anita

Running from the part of you that is the self and in circles leads us back to the truth. What is it that you want? What is it that you fear? Conflicts keep us trapped in false identity. Basically, we are multidimensional creatures caught between the linear nature of society and the asymmetrical nature of our personalities. Aligning our nature with our spirit takes courage. Stop fighting with your spirit, it can't hurt you. Your feelings, actions and thoughts are simply coming together. Find a common meeting ground within yourself to sort out your conflicts. We need to teach our young boys that it is okay to identify with their softer, vulnerable side without taking away from their masculine identity. The suppressed womb inflicts prejudice and many other harmful behaviors on society. My mother was a strong woman. She survived her womb trauma just as I have. I call her the "mighty rose" which just happens to be her name.

"The heart is a different language than the mind." – Anita

The rose is symbolic of love in that love occupies the inner space between two people in love which results in strength. It's about communicating from your intrinsic self.

"The heart does not understand hate." – Anita

Attention / Intention

To bear witness is part of the intention to attention. Attention is support of the inner world. Children require a lot of attention so the inner self is secure and develops properly. We all need attention and support for our own recreation and peace of mind. A lack of emotional attention ends up injuring the self. This is the time to turn your sights inward and reflect on your needs. What is it you want from yourself?

When we lack emotional nourishment, it means that we need to strengthen and stimulate our emotions so that we don't seek out negative, external forces. Inner attention is when we let go of the negative control the world and/or others have on us. When we let go of the negative, we realize the support of attention and are able to focus clearly. To be attentive requires receiving positive attention.

How much of your energy do you give away and how well do you function with the natural energy you have? Every relationship involves push and pull. One pushes, the other pulls and then there's an exchange where healthy boundaries are created. Awareness is the beginning of the creation of healthy boundaries. When we are in touch with our senses, we are able to clearly concentrate when and where to project our energy, thoughts and feelings. This equal exchange creates balance and harmony. Some of us need help in learning to give and receive. When our senses are open to the present moment, interchange automatically happens. If you do one without the other, the body tenses, forming defensive patterns. Before we know it, a psychological neediness develops. Practicing a healthy relationship with everyone is all it takes to avoid negative behaviors.

"Allow me to love you until you love yourself." – Anita

CHAPTER 2

༔

Opening My Heart to My Feelings

The Beat Goes On

"*I look at life for what it is; not for what I can get.*" – *Anita*

I have been writing for years with the driving force to get at least one book finished and into the hands of those of you who truly desire to change your lives for the better. With the entire world in such turbulence and my mother's passing, I have decided that now is a good time to share with you.

I'm going to start by telling you about the one person in my life who first steered me to the path of enlightenment—my mother. This woman was my role model and she lived a very difficult life. She couldn't find a way to let go of her pain and the conflicts that swirled around her like a fierce storm. Day in and day out, she struggled emotionally for love of the self, from others and the world. It all started with emotional trauma from an alcoholic father, an abusive husband, and my brother who was diagnosed with schizophrenia. She and my father divorced when I was 13 and my mother was left with four teenagers going in all directions.

Life in and of itself is challenging enough, so we must find happiness on our journey through life. Otherwise, life can be miserable for you and others around you just as it was for my mother, brother and I. My mother was one of the most unhappy, judgmental people I ever knew. It is because of her that I turned the negativity with which I was raised into happiness and love. My mother died at the age of 77. If anyone is in a better place, I know that she is. We either become like our role models or rise above, teaching others the difference between a life of suffering and a life of happiness and love. I celebrate the life she gave me and I challenge you to celebrate the life you have.

My life has had many different turns. I have gone from hardship, which turned into one experience after another. In essence, I have become the experiment, the test, the victim, the sufferer, the healer, the healed, the mother, the father, the white person, the black person, the cheater, the lover, the joker, the fool, the loner and the alone. My spirit has taken me through many lives and I'm sure it's not finished. I was once told that "I moved mountains".

The experiences we have are part of what we are doing today. Therefore, we need to honor every single one of them. Learning is what I do. Suffering is lessened each time the true self is expressed with regard to each experience.

> *"It's the moment of birth that stays with us forever—the love, the experience and the open heart." – Anita*

My re-birth encounter encouraged me to ask my mother about my pre-birth, as well as the birth itself. Surprised by my interest, she told me that she and my father had been separated near the time I was conceived and she was unsure if I was my father's child. This was the first I had heard of it. This uncertainty on my parent's part caused what was a disastrous time of extreme tension during my development in the womb.

Mother was very confused at the age of 26 and she attempted an abortion, which at the time was illegal. She inserted chemicals, but fortunately, was unsuccessful. I recalled experiencing disease when I was in a re-birth session and now I knew why. Mother also told me that I was the child she didn't want because of the separation she experienced with my father. I was the source of love that people so often push away. Unconsciously, she loved me and I loved me and that manifested into my actual birth. I was the cause of the conflict in the marriage.

When my father returned and found out about the pregnancy, they went right back to the same behavior—arguing. Perhaps that was a sign for them stating "quit while you're ahead." Instead, they ignored those signs and spent 21 years miserably married years—fighting the entire time. It was an extremely rocky road.

They divorced when I was 13 and just entering high school. It was a terrible time for them to finally call it quits. As teenagers, we require as much support from both parents as we can get. Many parents tend to think that teenagers are grown, when the truth is that we need them more than ever at that time.

My parents didn't see me when I became a teenager because they were so tightly bound by their own emotional turmoil. Essentially, I didn't receive enough love in the womb because my parents argued, emanating negative thoughts and feelings toward me before I was born. They lacked awareness and were not able to move from the path they were on. It's like looking at a picture and visualizing that scenario as being part of your life; how you stepped into it as well as how you're going to step out of it.

I was the problem and in the way, but my parents blamed each other. When two people hate each other, it's because they hate and disrespect themselves. They were standing at a crossroads when I came into the world. Due to a lack of awareness, they ended up crowding each other's personal boundaries. They blamed one another, leaving them each to search for an identity. Each had what I have come to call "the disease of hate." Unfortunately, that is the road that is easiest to take. They didn't understand emotional barriers and rawness because they were consumed with hate. It wasn't their fault; but rather a collective thought of negativity projecting into the world.

We all grow according to what we witness from observing the behavior of our parents. We also experience their transference. It is the love that we work hard to fulfill within ourselves. It is energy, whether negative or positive, between two parents that children learn to imitate. The heart is programmed with a different language than that of the mind. It's no wonder the heart and the mind often disagree. When we learn to connect the heart with the mind, we connect to the love we've been longing for.

According to my parent's backgrounds, they did share some common ground. They were both artists. Mother had studied drama, singing and dancing from the age of 10. Later, she cleaned houses to pay for her lessons. One of the most beautiful things about her was that she would sing to us. She sang to heal her soul and to cope with each moment in order to feel love and become closer to us.

My father restored antiques and was a cabinet maker. He drew patterns, carving them into the wooden structures making truly ornate pieces of furniture. He learned his craft from his father who had studied in Italy. His way of coping was to pour his creative self-expression into the wood and blocks he loved. One thing my mother always repeated was 'listen to your body.' It was this phrase that kept me open to the new things I was to learn.

I was in the third grade before it was discovered that my heart was diseased. Due to the constant conflict at home between my parents, there wasn't enough love for me. It was a harsh initiation of the spirit. I lived in a home and world that was full of chaos at a time when civilization was finding its way into western culture. I was emotionally sick from this family chaos. I was under-loved; therefore, my heart succumbed to a physical disease that stemmed from grating vibrations from memories that my muscles carried of my negative experience in the womb. This negative in-trauterine experience and the family chaos combined to allow for this ill-ness to happen. My heart couldn't take it, so my body's immune system shut down in complete suppression and was overcome by disease. Disease forms from a lack of love; it goes away when you start to love.

This internal crisis peaked one cold December afternoon in 1966. I contracted rheumatic fever, which begins with strep throat and often leaves the heart damaged, by affecting the connective tissue. I was left with a faulty valve in my heart that allowed the blood to flow backward into the left chambers of the heart. Due to this, my heart didn't pump enough blood through my body. Medical technology has advanced to the point that rheumatic fever is now a thing of the past. I learned that the famous Joseph Pilates experienced the same disease of rheumatic fever which also encouraged him to get involved with the body as well. He died in 1967. The sixties were the tail end of this disease.

Doctors told my parents that I was going to die just as other children with my condition, inevitably, did. Back then, children of lower income families often contracted these types of illnesses, many of them dying from them. I was admitted to the hospital where I stayed for six months. It was during this time that I, subconsciously, discovered a way to escape the hate and sorrow that was the chaos in my family and the world. *I wanted to save myself.* This disease could have easily stolen my life like it had done with so many others that I had witnessed, but I had one very important thing going for me. I was determined to live. This surge of strength was in me just waiting to live on. I stayed alive one heart beat at a time. Since I had a strong will to live and valued life, I learned to overcome the disease and survived this traumatic turning point in my journey. I opened my heart-of-no- love until I began to love the hate that surrounded me. With this attitude, I cured my heart disease. From that point on, I chose life. Sadly, many people don't and, as a result, they slowly die.

I was raised in a middle class Italian family in Philadelphia. With the constant bickering between my parents, I would often go elsewhere to escape the turmoil and seek the love I so desperately needed. Unfortunately, I couldn't run from it all the time and was an unwilling witness to the emotional and physical abuse. This tension never left our home environment until they divorced. My father often used his fists on my mother as though she was a human punching bag as men still do today even though women have come a long way. The sickening sound of his fist making contact with her body and her tears was unendurable at times. But, it was a man's way of taking control when he couldn't exercise his ego with others of his temperament in the world.

It was a terrible hardship for me to come home daily, facing a traumatic environment that was almost the norm of the way people thought in the world at that time. The emotions I experienced, led me to behave poorly. It was these emotional upheavals that caused my heart to become ill. I never learned how to express love and rarely ever received it. Consciously I wanted to, but internally it was difficult. The dysfunctional family environment left me emotionally underdeveloped. It's as if my heart became ill in order to force me to stop and deal with this crucial need. Even though my heart hadn't been properly nourished in the womb, ironically, this would lead to my discovery of love. I made a choice that included learning and re-learning my lifestyle.

I was nine years old when I was unnaturally exposed to the hardships of life. This was when my body went into the ups and downs of physical suffering. It was during this time in life that I learned about emotions, that they can be beautiful as well as uncomfortable. When I experienced stress, I realized that I could become emotionally sick much the same as if I had a stomachache. I began to treat my emotions as if they were a physical part of my body.

This learning took place during the six long months I spent in Children's Heart Hospital (CHH) in Philadelphia. It was a hospital strictly for children afflicted with heart and asthma challenges. CHH was also a long distance from home, so my parents could only come on weekends to visit me.

I learned all about the extremes of 'hot and cold,' both physically and emotionally and what it meant in accordance with achieving internal balance. First, I had learned the emotional side of coldness when it came to life at home. This lesson was one incident that occurred just before I became so ill. It happened on a winter day, when my father was so upset and angry that he picked me up, sat me out on the cold steps with a suitcase, and locked me out of the house for approximately ten minutes. It was a very long ten minutes and I suffered overwhelming feelings of abandonment. Having no choice, I took those moments and faced the cold, both physically and emotionally. I turned away from the door, allowing myself to associate the nature of cold air with the coldness of the human spirit, and on occasion, life. I realized that cold weather was very similar to a lack of human affection—a lack of love. I also realized that weather was a tool that nature provided in order for me to become familiar with my spiritual life.

"In every moment of suffering, I saw an opening to let go of the pain:
I transformed right there in the moment" – Anita

Separation

Lying in the hospital bed helped me prepare for the world, for life, for death and for love. I felt what I thought it must have been like being adrift on a lifeboat while watching the Titanic sink. While I was there, I never knew if I was going to live or die. Being separated from the rest of the world was challenging yet meditative after a while. I began learning to separate from the thoughts and noises in my head. This separated me from my ego, and as a result, became a tool that helped me get out of my own way, so that I could face the challenges that lay ahead of me. It was a blessing in disguise.

My imagination became quite vivid. I would see my body moving and my feet walking in my dreams. I imagined that life was the most beautiful place in the world. By keeping that alive in my imagination, it made me believe that, one day I would get out of that bed and move again. The separation from my family served to build an inner strength and independence that showed me the God inside. I was caught between two wars, the war of the roses at home, and the war in the hospital. There was nowhere to turn, but "in." In order to find peace and love, I discovered the love inside of me that I had been missing from my parents. I made this a conditioned behavior for me. Inwardly, I became my own "parents" and, whereby, loved myself.

> *"I was lying in my hospital bed when the feeling of divinity came into me." – Anita*

The Turmoil of Racism

When I first entered the institution I felt lost and was often left alone. The day I arrived, I was wheeled in a wheelchair to a glass cabinet filled with dolls. I was told to pick a doll. I picked a Mary Hoyer doll that I kept at my bedside. This doll represented my self esteem. She went through the good times as well as the bad times with me. Each time I looked at her, I felt renewed strength. That doll helped me hold onto life. From that time forward, I never saw dolls as play things again. That doll held an exalted position in my surroundings. She represented where I was going as well as remembering from whence I came and it all began.

The hospital only loaned me the doll. When I left, after six months, they wanted her back. I fought with them to keep her. How could they do something so cruel to a child? As they continued to wheel me down the hall to my bed, I kept repeating to myself, *"I want to live."*

The next place they put me was in an all girl ward. I was the only white child among African American children. They were suffering from severe illnesses too.

This part of my hospital stay led to a time of social awareness outside my own ethnic family heritage. All at once, I was faced with youthful racism in this wing of the hospital. Racial tensions and riots had flared up across the country in the early 1960's, creating a trend for hatred in that decade.

My desperate desire to get out of my hospital bed and move around associated with the peoples' desire, at that time, to move and progress socially. My little moves, "undulations," to establish my space and self-expression were parallel to what was going on all over the country. Little movements often bring about big ones; which bring about change. I was synchronized in time with those vital social movements.

Being the only white girl surrounded by colored children gave me a feeling of being one of them. At least I could empathize, since it wasn't a good time in the world for them. I grabbed hold of the pieces they sometimes shared of their souls. Most of the time, I was subject to taunts, and rude/abusive gestures from them. I never blamed them. They were just reacting to what white America handed them. In time I learned to turn my anger into love for these kids. It was the love that saved my soul and my health.

"From hate to love was a beautiful journey to learn.
It took a lot of courage for me to go there." – Anita

When I was being ridiculed and abused by the black girls, I suffered. I really endured change and struggle as much as they did, because I was in white America. I was making my own path toward freedom according to my own feelings. I experienced a profound change from resistance to willpower and finally truth in the space of one moment out of time. It was from this change that I found my inborn strength.

"Strength comes from love." – Anita

At first it was simply culture shock. Black and white people didn't mingle or play together at that time. White people would walk out of a store if black people were in it. It was that bad. Neither did our races mix well enough to make a happy team. As children, we didn't understand, so we gave up parts of our growth as children, to satisfy the needs of world politics. It's no wonder that adults have so much pain and there lots of mentally challenged people in society these days.

"I found God because my desire for life was so strong." – Anita

I was just as shut out as the black kids, due in part to the fact that the world was full of prejudice, hate and suffering. So, for the first four months, I endured being ridiculed and physically attacked. They would call me "whitey" as they took turns hitting me. Still, I didn't blame them.

I blamed the world. To look only at the world I was in would have been ignorant. Being part of everything and everyone had helped me sort out and understand what was happening. There were times I would call the nurses to stop the abuse I suffered and their sufferings as well, but they didn't want to have anything to do with it. Prejudice had brain washed white America.

I was terribly ill with fevers of 105 degrees every day and all I could do was crawl into my shell and hide. I thought I had found a way out from beneath my dysfunctional family noise. Instead, I learned we can't run away from our problems. We must face our challenges head on, one by one. This takes courage; the kind of courage that comes from the heart. I had, subconsciously, created the separation from my family chaos, only to find myself fighting another war. I considered myself the wise child who managed to get away from the family war. I realized a need to get away from the racial war or I would die from my heart disease for sure. *I had to find a way to love. I was suffering from not knowing how to love myself.*

Until I found the 'undulations' which were a fluid movement of love in my body, I endured. The other kids were suffering just as the world was. Unfortunately, the world continues to suffer today. I asked for a social worker, but the nurse denied me. When my parents visited, it was never for very long and when they left, I would stand at the window watching them go away and cry. I felt abandoned. I would wave goodbye until I could no longer see them. I had no choice, so I learned patience. As a result of the love I had discovered inside myself, I honored my soul.

During my stay at CHH, I began to understand what "being in the alone" was all about. I spent a lot of time alone. My loneliness caused a separation of part of myself. I had to branch off from the center of myself in order to find the help that I needed to get well. I would lie in my bed and undulate my body. This was when I started to feel my "presence."

I wanted to get out of the caged bed I was in, where there were no privileges. CHH was run like an army boot camp. There were tags on my bed dictating what I could and couldn't do. I would lie there and close my eyes. First I used to kick and move uncontrollably, because I desperately wanted out. I left my family to be confined in another way.

Essentially, we make our own 'jails' from the way we have been molded since our childhood, often lasting our lifetime. I didn't want that, so I continued to move and my movements became slower and more fluid —a wave-like motion that allowed me to feel alive. This undulating fluidity was a movement of love for me. Love is an instinctual concept of our selves. This is where the undulation originated. Our body's natural movement is a wave-like movement.

"My undulations were a movement of love." – Anita

My heart needed love, so this was the beginning of the creation of a love relationship with me. I found a way out of the suffering by turning inward and loving myself. When we truly learn to love ourselves, we will never hate anyone. We learn to let go of the judgements. My levels of consciousness were and still are very high. This is why I had a hard time going through life. It takes people half a lifetime to get to the conscious level of reason, acceptance, and neutrality etc.

God made himself known to me through my feelings during my alone time. I was consciously moving though the fluids of my body. This led to stabilizing and connecting to my chakras,* or energies within. I had finally found a way to love myself. This brought great joy for me—a joy that would last me the rest of my life.

"When we find the love of the self, we have everything." – Anita

I was fortunate enough to have made this discovery at the age of nine. I am a living experiment; therefore, I want to share with you this wealth of joy. I healed myself by moving through my body, not knowing that my chakras were getting stimulated. I didn't know what chakras were at the time. With the movements, my immune system took care of itself. Thus, I discovered that we can heal ourselves using our own natural powers of love. When you're in your conscious truth love has no detour.

"Love is a fire, but whether it's going to warm your heart or burn down your house, you can never tell." – Joan Crawford

How I Taught Myself to Love Me
"If you have yourself, you can go anywhere and be anybody, and no one will care, because you're the only one watching"
– Anita

I found the love within me through the undulation of my body. I trained myself to open my heart while undulating according to my feelings. This allowed my thoughts to open so that I could love those around me. It was by opening to love, that my immune system was strengthened sufficiently enough to attack the rheumatic fever. This, over time, effectively cured me. Due to the fact that I could not get out of bed, I would lie there moving my pelvis—squirming for all I was worth. This turned into an evolving undulation whereby, my entire body began to experience a build-up of energy, breath and fluidity. This continuous activity moved through my body to my heart. While in that horrible bed, I would move my body, switching between symmetrical and asymmetrical movements. It was a combination of my own discoveries and the treatments by the medical staff that cured me. I suffered with 105 degree temperatures over a course of four months. Those high temperatures, along with the undulations I was doing, softened the important connective fascia tissue *(CFT). You're only as young as your connective tissue is flexible. You're only as young as your spine is movable.

All illnesses stem from unhealthy cells. When we become aware of the basis of this; diseases can be easily prevented. The goal, with therapy and exercise is to improve and promote healthy cells. If I hadn't discovered my particular undulated movements, I would have died. It was the realization of this presence that, ultimately, cured me.

> *"Moments there were in fiery red and all I could see was the burning fevered bed." – Anita*

Hydrotherapy

What also helped me to acquire knowledge and the ability to self-heal, were the hydrotherapy treatments I received for my high fevers. Every night for six months, the nurses came in with buckets of ice. I felt so dry; I can only describe it by saying, the hell in my body died when I got into that ice. That blessed cold took all the burning hell out of my soul. It was through these ice baths that I rejuvenated and became a clean soul. I considered it purification by fire and ice. Those tubs were so cold that I felt like I was in them for an eternity. I would sit there alone and shivering. I had to find a way to escape this miserable feeling that kept me locked up physically and emotionally. It was this loneliness that caused me to venture forth and discover my own world. My spirit created a new life and that is what I'm living today. I was always wondering when the misery would all come to an end. There were no parents to comfort me and no friendly hospital friends to commiserate with. A loss of love only recognizes hate. Is it possible to end the suffering?

It is this balance of hot and cold, when applied to the muscles and connective tissues, that enhances one's forgiveness of the soul. My entire hospital stay initiated a healing baptism, re-birth—newness. I learned to use my imagination to shift from the bed and become the shadow I saw on the wall. This shadow became my friend. In times of fear and loneliness, children learn to create imaginary friends to help them through the rough times in life. All these new experiences came together for me in the ice tub where I experienced and achieved physical and emotional balance. I developed pranayama; which is the life force that we achieve when practicing yoga. The life force within was what gave me my hope and faith to go on.

"Life for me is a gift. I've been pardoned; granted elegance."
– Anita

I realized that my heart had only so much love. This was due, of course, to the lack of it in my home environment. Therefore, I needed to breathe new life into my heart. Lying in my bed, all I could hear was my heart beating in my head and I would think that "the beat will go on." It was around that time when pop duo Sonny and Cher hit it big with the song, *The Beat Goes On.* Its' simple lyrics were a profound statement about how life moves on, one beat after another. Soon, the love I had for myself overpowered my thoughts. I didn't care whether or not I was liked, or what other people thought of me. I just wanted to live; and I managed this from purifying and opening my heart to my own feelings. My thoughts never deviated from the path of life. Love took me away from it all.

"As I lay in my bed, all I could hear was the heartbeat in my head."
– Anita

When I finally emerged from my bed six months later, I had to learn how to move my body all over again. I felt old and beat up; shriveled. But my young muscles had undergone a drastic change. When I looked into my eyes in the mirror, they appeared to be the eyes of an older, more experienced person, one who had journeyed through an entire life. This strange new person I had become had gained knowledge and understanding. When I moved, all of my expressions surfaced; my movements were somewhat like the actions of a mime. This is the way I functioned due to the mental scars that had developed.

I began to recreate this therapeutic action with the help of my body and, ironically, with the help of the black kids in the hospital that danced so freely around me. This series of movements became my tool for self-expression. It was as though I had lived an entire lifetime in that hospital. I had experienced love, war, peace, stillness, darkness, light, freezing cold and searing heat all in the space of six months.

"I have become one with the weather." – Anita

Pain is a Source of Information

Although I experienced a lot of illness, I didn't fight it. Instead, I embraced it and it became my teacher instead of my enemy. By going with it and finding the love within, is how I healed. The disease that ravaged my body was just a set of troubled emotions which developed from the part of me that had been stressed. We need to have the courage to dive in and ask for help. I started to view my pain and emotional stress as information.

Disease springs from emotional negativity, and the pain it gives is also emotional. It's this emotional well-being that we need to listen to. Pay attention to those inner voices and get rid of the negative parent-like voice inside you that attempts to make you hate yourself. Inside the vast warehouse of your brain is where the information is stored. So the next pain you get, ask yourself these questions: What do I need? What do I want from myself? What am I not getting enough of? What is bothering me?

"I was faced with life and death in every moment. Suffering is your spiritual teacher...evolve" – Anita

My mother told me that I had cried so much when I was in the hospital that, in later years, I hardly cried at all. I think I cried all my tears in those six months because I had no other way to let my emotions out until I discovered "undulations." Since that experience, I have always been interested in the body; the way it moves, the way it communicates when it is stressed, and the way it cries out when it has needs.

"My emotions undulated like the wave" –Anita

My tears were real then and long-lasting. I cried much as the bereaved do when someone in the family has died. I was grieving for myself that had not yet begun to live. I cried for life, for fear, and for love. For me, the tears represented the water in my body. They represented freedom and flow. When the ice soaks surrounded my body, it was almost like being back in the womb, only much colder. Maybe I was regressing to that point in order to reenact those old emotions that had been born with me. I was trapped within an emotional prison of my own making. Even the bed I lay in had two prison-like bars that physically kept me isolated.

When I was finally allowed to get out of bed, I experienced my feelings move through my body, (thoughted motion.) This is when I discovered that the body retains memories; that your muscles and tissues remember everything that has ever occurred. My feelings were stored deep in my body and begged to be expressed. I related to my emotions as if they were another person's body language—expressed according to the movements of the world. Even though I was only nine, I understood the language of the body.

"Freedom equates to the movement of life." – Anita

Coming Out of Isolation
"I gotta move!" – Anita

The first words out of my mouth when I was released from the sick bed were; *"I gotta move, I gotta move!"* I couldn't stop moving. It was a wonderful privilege to just get up and be able to walk around. Then I was allowed to go to the recreation room, the classroom, and the dining room areas. In the recreation area, I became a bit of a pool shark. From all the wisdom I gained while imprisoned in my bed, I developed the center of me and found my direction. The game of pool helped me with focus.

At nine years of age, children still function from instinct. It's not until after we're grown and are shaped and molded, that we lose some of that. So, we need to stay in touch with our feelings in order to validate and gain our sense of self. After being fed, tutored and potty trained in bed, it was time for my life to begin anew. This is when I got in touch with my primal self, my animal instinct. Isolation had become a regular emotion. I knew that place—that emptiness well. At times I had felt as if I were locked up in Alcatraz, in solitary confinement. Just being able to walk to and use the toilet was a special privilege.

It was during this time that my hospital mates and I became friends. Those black kids would be dancing and doing their usual rhythmic moves. Now, I was able to move with them, not wanting to stop. We came together in peace through the dance, celebrating our lives. The rhythmic dance we shared turned into happiness and, eventual friendship. In spite of life with its ups and downs, we became friends. I was ahead of my time— ahead of the world. I was "who's coming to dinner".

With isolation, what happens after awhile is that you wake up one day and desire to "move past who you are." You've been fighting with yourself for years. Then, suddenly, the ego dissolves and you can't hold on anymore, so you surrender, realizing there never was a period of isolation, only ignorance. When you feel isolated, it's because you're not allowing yourself to connect with your feelings. When you do connect and are able to acknowledge your feelings, your heart opens and you are able to reach out to another and share life. It is the strength in being resilient.

"Let go of the isolation and create a life – Teach yourself." – Anita

Philosophies & Lessons Learned from Chapter 2

Philosophies

If we hold onto negative emotions and anger, they will eventually manifest as disease or violence.

In Africa, they do drumming rituals for the pregnant woman as a way of life. This stimulates rhythm and regularity of the senses and opens the body to its fluid nature.

The more we don't accept about ourselves, the more we decrease our life patterns and much-needed experiences.

Control in any way is oppression, even if someone is joking. There's discipline and there's control, but they are different. In today's world, men are coming to a deeper level of understanding within themselves; they are learning to harness their feminine nature as women do their masculine nature, but we still have a long way to go.

Unfortunately, when children are exposed to family challenges, they have to learn what love is all over again. The where, when and how is a human condition. The process could take a lifetime. With all the interventions available to us today, it could certainly be done much quicker.

We need to come together within ourselves first, then collectively with each other.

Separation revolves around adjustment and how to intrinsically adjust. Separation from the ego was a big part of the moment for me and from attachment of the things in life that didn't really matter. I made an authentic connection toward my truth. This feeling of separation led me to a place separate from my body and mind. I found the voice of love and for years people put me down, but what I realized is what they couldn't face in themselves. Love is an emotion of patience and depth. Give yourself this kind of love.

The world seemed divided between blacks and whites. Race riots had erupted bitterly in the heart of Philadelphia. Movement was a word that stuck in my head then, because the 60's were defined in terms of movements, i.e. the civil rights movement and the peace movement.

From what I know today, I was moving my sex and heart chakras and healing myself by opening up these energies. My kundalini energy was being stimulated and an ascension of a flow which thrived through my spine up to my head.

Immobility is death for fascia. A hard body is not a healthy body. The body needs to be strong, yet fluid in nature. When we lose the liquid nature, the body is more susceptible to disease. The masculine and feminine within each of us need to join forces. The masculine is the grounding muscle while the feminine is the creative connective tissue. This is one of the reasons why exercise is so important these days and cross training is crucial.

The hydrotherapy was the beginning of my "prana buildup." Through this experience I have developed my Shakti. The kundalini or otherwise known as chi energy had risen and opened my central nervous system, which helped in developing the prana life force energy.

The sacred temple of divine is a means to conquer death. My past negative karma was leaving my body. In India, yogis practice the cold and hot treatment to enhance their wisdom, to learn about the inner mind. This is how they develop a positive life force. They may sit in Ashrams in the hot or spend hours meditating in the cold.

Lessons Learned

It was my diseased heart that taught me about love. It is the organ of love. Stress and a lack of love affect the hearts normal rhythm. It is at the very core of life.

During my hospital stay, I learned to cultivate internal power and wisdom and eventually learned to protect my heart from further illness and vulnerability. I learned from a young age that if I didn't take charge of my life, no one else would. I learned it is basically up to each and every one of us to care for ourselves.

I've learned to differentiate, giving me the ability to see things in a different light. Separation taught me to self-identify and categorize my thinking which helps me to compartmentalize my thoughts. When we categorize our thinking, its part of balancing out our lives. Separation teaches us boundaries and this is what I needed. Separation revolves around adjustment and how to adjust.

Being locked into my hospital bed, I learned all about how we are suffering and living in our own mental jails—how we create the "rock and a hard place." This is why I am a free spirit today because I learned to get out of the mental jail that gets in the way from a young age. I built a foundation.

After much spiritual training, I realized that we are responsible for every experience and that we subconsciously place ourselves there so that we can learn what our dharma is.

I learned that my body was moving from instinct and my sensory stimulators created the impulses, sending messages to my brain cells. My connective fascia tissue was at the source of all healing.

To have healthy CFT, the body needs to stretch and move. This helps to prevent disease. The fascia helps hold the body upright, creating "cables" that provide lift and movement.

The reality is within and that I've learned to be myself through the lives of others.

Last Minute Advice
Stop Complaining!

For every time you complain, I want you to look in the mirror and be thankful that you can complain. Be thankful that there are things to complain about. Be thankful that you can voice your complaints. Then I want you to take notice of how beautiful you are. Complaining does not exist on the plane of love. Change planes for a day or two, step back and see the difference. Make a mental note to do this. When we complain it is a cry for help. The help we cry out for is the love we desire and deserve so desperately. When we complain, we remain in the victim mentality.

Trivia

As applies to rhythm. The Tarantula spider dance became famous in Taranto Italy in the 15th century. Tarantism was a disease once thought to result from the bite of the tarantula spider. The affliction was associated with the following symptoms: Melancholy, stupor, desperation, madness, and an uncontrollable desire to dance. The dancing was violent and highly energetic, lasting from three to four days. They danced to free themselves, to free their expression. Alessandra Belloni of New York teaches a fiery percussive journey through the south of Italy in her "rhythm is the cure" workshops where they do the trance dance called the Pizzica Tarantata which is used to cure the mythical bite of evil that leeches into our subconscious mind that can keep us in a suppressed state of negativity; thus living in an emotional underworld.

CHAPTER 3

❧

Let Go of the Victimization

"The challenge was to see how much 'like' I could get out of myself."
–Anita

Just what does it mean to let go of victimization? Some of the things I've heard others say that keep them holding on are: They will be punished because they did some bad things and so on. Cleaning the karma regularly helps the mind to get pure again.

These are the inner thoughts and worlds of people that live with victimization and self doubt—who live in the gutter of humanity. In the world of today, we have come a long way so that this inner thinking is considered "old hat." But, we still punish ourselves needlessly. They will be punished because they did some bad things and so on. Cleaning the karma regularly helps the mind to get pure again. We can choose to learn from our mistakes or continue making them

Many times, the mistake is a blessing in disguise. When we learn from our mistakes, we become enlightened and empowered. We can teach others what it is that has blossomed from that seed. I took every mistake I made, learned from them, and became better for it.

"Get up off the couch." – Sherelle P. Johnson
Let go of the victimization. You owe it to yourself!" – Anita

My illness was the beginning of what was to come in my life. I was a victim and so were the other kids. Everyone is a victim at one time or another. If you've ever seen the movie The Secret, then you are familiar with the victim mindset—letting go of the negative stuff that binds others —that lives in you. The key is not to live in or with the pain of others.

Many times we tend to take on the burdens of others and make it a part of us, which can and often leads to emotional pain. Once you are able to take charge and let go of being the victim, you will be able to live freely and with happiness. Holding on to burdens of any kind creates stress; that temporarily relieves pain, but blocks necessary feelings. People suffer because they are waiting for others to deliver them—looking for a personal savior. My personal advice to you is; "Get up off the couch and take charge!"

I used my fight against loneliness to become someone special. Instead of falling into the role of the victim and waiting for someone to save me, I pulled myself from the fire. This is what we all need to do; take charge and responsibility for your own life—stop crying and holding on.

It took a serious illness in my heart, watching other children die, and being involved in racial wars while in the hospital to understand that, with the love I created, I was able to rise from the diversity and heal myself.

I learned to separate from my pain by changing my way of thinking so that I would live. I made a promise to myself, as a child, to do whatever it takes to have the right to my life. Think back on the promises you made yourself as a child. Did you follow through? Do you still want to? I'm here to tell you that you can! It's just a matter of letting go of the fear.

"Without mistakes, we can't forgive or learn." – Anita

Then there is prejudice. I felt rejected by white America because I was dealing with the same self-esteem issues as the black kids. I remember asking my mom on one of their visits. "Why don't white people allow their kids to play with black kids?" She didn't have an answer.

I had experienced, first hand, the hurt and anger black people felt because they were not accepted in white society. My life ran parallel to this because, during most of it, I never felt accepted either. It was for different reasons, but the effects are similar. I learned a lot about human nature—how we are all one, due to the basic emotions we share.

"No one is free when others are oppressed." – Anita

Being accepted has been a big challenge most of my life. On every occasion when I didn't feel accepted by family or friends, I identified with the black kids I had known in the hospital. Abuse is something the world is just coming to terms with, as well as feelings of the alienation that lies behind it. Due to the fact that I was different, I faced the challenge of being accepted in groups. So, where did I fit in?

Nowhere, and I was ridiculed most of my life because of it. I wasn't even accepted within the alien cultures that surrounded me. Who was it that said; "Sticks and stones may break my bones but words can never harm me?" I never heard such an untrue statement. Yet this was the only defense against ridicule, which is really a poor weapon for people to hide behind. Ridicule hurts all the way to the core because it separates us into physical, superficial categories.

"I look toward life, not at it." – Anita

I believe that racism was included as part of human nature for a reason. Perhaps it's God's way of teaching us to symbolically see the true meaning of light and dark, their complimentary aspects and how they represent in yin and yang. They are opposites therefore, they complement each other.

We need night and day; one is black, the other white. Yet night and day are two different sides of a 24 hour calendar period. One cannot exist without the other. It isn't surprising that the two most favored flavors of ice cream are chocolate and vanilla. How absurd prejudice seems when you can compare it to the color of food.

"Every moment was a moment of life—a reason to live."– Anita

To look at life is to be dissatisfied with it, but to look toward life is to appreciate it. Looking toward life keeps us in the present moment.

I began to view racial challenges as an unfortunate expression of society's needs. I felt enlightened when I saw the differences between my colored friends, not only in the color of our skin, but in the emotions and the every day events that we shared. Looking toward life teaches us to have a greater acceptance of the different cultures in the world. It also teaches us to accept people who are mentally challenged, whether due to a genetic heritage or a traumatic event. Children who are retarded as well as those with multi-ethnic backgrounds are placed in this world so that we can learn to join together, harmoniously, in order that our mistakes may be minimal, and not repeated. It's about being able to accept yourself for who you are and what you do. Then it becomes easier to "live and let live." If we truly accept ourselves, we don't waste valuable time looking for the faults in other people.

People crushed me for 'being me.' A perfect example would be the character Kevin Spacey portrayed in the movie American Beauty. The movie is about the dark side of an American family, about the nature and price of beauty in a culture obsessed with outward appearances and the toll it takes.

There are other people who have been condemned for being who they were and expressing what they believed in. Some of them are: Margaret Mead, Karen Silkwood, Harvey Milk, Martin Luther King, Eleanor Roosevelt, Abby Hoffman, Joan of Arc, Dr. Wilhelm Reich, pop singer Madonna and radio jock Howard Stern. They are all examples of people who enjoy themselves enough that they share their differences with the world—entertaining them as well.

My Story Continued
"I know how to grab life like a ball.
But I wouldn't throw it, it's too precious." – Anita

I had the unfortunate sorrow, during my hospital stay, to have witnessed the deaths of other children. This was another profound experience in my young life. I especially remember one girl in particular. She had a bad case of asthma and her family was preparing to move to Arizona where the air was dryer, so that she could breathe easier. Sadly, her spirit couldn't hold out long enough to make the trip. It was a terrible truth that several children didn't make it through their illnesses.

I watched, with trepidation, as bodies were wrapped and taken away. With both mystified curiosity and anguish, I wondered if I would be one of them. This unknown factor was a daily roller coaster for my unstable emotions.

One of the best things about my stay was that children from my school wrote to me, in order to keep close, give encouragement, and stay connected. This distant love became symbolic in my life. I began writing them back and loved receiving their mail. I received stacks of mail from these kids—so many fan letters arrived, that I started to believe I was special. The nuns encouraged the children to write to me. It was a bright ray of sunshine in the dark and dismal surroundings, and I still have those encouraging letters.

While I lay in the hospital bed, my body began to feel strangely mechanical. I was denied any real movement. After so much of the enforced immobility, getting out of bed and moving became challenging for me. Later on, I became very athletic. I took on the challenge of physical sports with zeal. The doctors had told me, while I was young, that I couldn't do anything strenuously physical, but I proved them wrong and continued with my self-imposed course of athletics. I was infused with power from my own insight and the doll that meant so much to me. My immune system was so severely suppressed that I retreated into the silence of my soul. Later, I took up swimming because of this.

Authority, Illness & Culture
"Every moment grants us a chance to relive." – Anita

I was provided with a tutor to teach me the fourth-grade assignments I was missing while in the hospital. If her words and finger pointing gestures could kill, I was surely going to die.

The woman was terrifying and very abusive—like an overwhelming, scary firestorm that threatened my little aura of light. She utilized verbal abuse like it was a weapon and attacked me with it every week. She used negative body gestures to expel pent-up feelings that lay beneath her skin. That finger kept pointing at me and appeared to stretch far enough to bruise my already damaged emotions of inferiority that were rapidly developing. I cried the entire time—six long months of that horror.

I was angry, but also scared of that woman. I saw her pain, her daily misery and her intentional mistrust. Today, I know why "superior" feels more like "inferior" to me. I never learned the trait of being able to look up to someone and appreciate that person as an authority figure, a teacher—guider. I'm still working on it, though. Instead, I looked up to my tutor and wanted to kill her. I couldn't look at her as an authority figure, so I became my own leader, instead of her victim. Her attitude helped me develop my own inner strength. As a result I developed leadership capabilities, and tuned into an awareness of my own. Of course, my ego became over-developed, but later I learned to let down my defenses. My tutor intentionally oppressed me. She knew what she was doing and so did I and she was aware that I knew it. It didn't stop her, though. Children are aware and see these things in the makings.

Due to her abusive, selfish, hateful nature, I developed feelings in my own mind that worked against me. My higher power couldn't equalize on a level with her cruel authority. It was a tough and lonely time for me. Eventually, I was given the nickname, "mother superior," because of my assertiveness. I had to become my own leader or I would have died. This put me in a unique situation with others later in my life especially going through girlhood. I became a monster in my own right, but I developed "presence," which supports my spirit. *Nourishing your spirit brings about the joy in every emotion.*

I was just a scared little girl wanting out of my padded prison. There was nowhere to go and no one to talk to. Instead, the oppression I felt made me want to free who I was, rather than turn inward and hide. There was so much hate around me; between the tutor and the kids who didn't know any better, the unfriendly nurses and parents who were unaware, and as always, my diseased heart. All I could find was me. So, I saved myself, alone in the dark. I'm not afraid of the dark and lonely; it is actually where I go to re-charge.

When fear sinks its claws into our souls, our life force can be beaten down. Then depression occurs. Every ending gives us a chance to re-live again, better than before, especially in our relationships. Because of my tutor's abusive conduct, I couldn't grasp any of the work she wanted me to do. She emotionally overwhelmed me. I know when I am treated with kindness because I am touched and remember instruction, therefore communicating better. I dealt with the awful experience by looking straight ahead. I wanted life more. I wanted out of the hospital so badly that it became one of my more powerful motivators. I was a slave to the conflicts of the world, just as a lot of people are. We tend to become slaves under the leaders that govern our society—to politics of all kinds— the media and crime etc.

"I live for love because I forgave myself." – Anita

I live for love only because I learned forgiveness. I accept people as they are. If they are angry and abusive, even toward me, I choose to accept them anyway. If I was going to heal my illness, I needed to forgive and so the spirit of forgiveness came into me. Once I forgave myself for being born into the mess my family was, I could forgive others and start spreading love to the world around me. In essence I created the life of my dreams and you can to. Isn't that what life is really all about?

"I didn't have to create a false personality or wear a mask, because I didn't have to face anyone." – Anita

Oppression can be turned into something positive, if you are open-minded. I had to accept the situation in the hospital, as unpleasant as it was, in order to survive both physically and emotionally. It was just another challenge for me. I used undulated movements to break from my oppressors, not only from my bed, but from my emotionally damaged self. Those six, seemingly endless, months in CHH actually taught me how to be me. Because I was alone, I talked to myself and could only be "the real me." I developed the "presence" part of me. Basically, I was alone in my own little drama. People with false personalities are the way they are so they don't have to face who they are. The real me is where I stayed. The core of my heart is where I claim my being resides. By locking in energy, I unlocked my brain. When we can face ourselves, we can face anything.

"All of my energy was stored in the body, just waiting to live."– Anita

Time in a Bottle

Some of the more pleasant memories of my hospital stay were the fairs. This was when all the parents and children came together. They were similar to county fairs in a way. One boy and one girl each was chosen to receive a wrist watch for being the "Most Outstanding Patient." On one such unforgettable occasion, I was chosen by the God that exists in all of us and, to this day, I still have that watch. For me, that endearing gift of recognition signified life—the living connection of the moments we call living, and how life represents time.

The watch was silver and black and fit perfectly around my little wrist. At such a youthful stage in my life, I began and developed a belief system deep within. I granted myself success by demonstrating freedom. The watch was a symbolic verification that I was achieving the freedom I so desperately wanted. I was finally given special attention—I was "outstanding." I had come into my own and, for the rest of my life, I've stood out.

Who invented time? If there were no clocks, life would never run out. So, this is what the watch signified for me—that my life would never run out; as if it was stored like a bottle of wine, fermenting and growing into its perfection, only to be born over and over again. Take a closer look at those you are giving your precious time to. Preserve each moment and take pride with what time you are given.

> *"To heal is to be thyself. To survive is to live on the edge.*
> *To experience life is to be. I am a whole being." – Anita*

On my Way Home; Silence of the Heart

I was finally on my way home. The feeling of excitement, over going home, wrapped around my healed heart like a warm blanket. My father picked me up. I was no longer ill and on my way home—the new "me." It was such a good feeling to be going home after six long, miserable months. This was one of the most exciting days of my life.

Just before I left, I had gone to say goodbye to little Julia. She was there due to severe Asthma and was a year older than me. She was always so fragile, but cheerful. Her parents were there because she was having one of her attacks. Unfortunately, it was to be her last one. I cradled her lovingly in my arms only to say goodbye, but she died as I held her. It was at this point that I knew life was a gift for me. It's as if God spoke in that moment and said, "You have a chance, little one—run, run, run for life."

This last sad occasion was also one of my life's treasured moments. My entire hospital stay had been heart-wrenching in more ways than what was obvious. It was the beginning of the challenges in my life. I remember how Julia's parents looked at me—accusingly, as if I was lucky for having survived. That look was also accompanied with sadness, hate, love, hurt and jealousy. I witnessed the entire spectrum of emotions that went through them in that moment when they realized their baby girl was dead.

Even today, I feel people always look at me like I have it all together and have everything. I do because I value life. What I have, is a unique feeling of happiness that I carry around while I'm here on earth—alive. In essence it's those same people that came from better families that looked away, turning to the outside world for happiness.

I may have been unfortunate, but I survived and prevailed. I would have rather come from the best foundation that love can bring. Everyone would. However, I'm blessed and happy with the gift of my life. For me, it was hate and oppression all along the way, but with all that hate directed at and around me, I still turned and chose to love. I was lucky, as some would say, but I also had a lot going for me. I had a determination to live. That's better odds than playing and winning the lottery. Today, other people still see that determination shining forth from me.

There is a song by jazz artist, Carmen McRae, called *The Precious Right to Love*. It reminds me of how I felt after little Julia died in my arms. Love is not a privilege, but a right. I give back to life and this is how I express my "attitude of gratitude" for my gifts. What will you choose? Love or hate? If you choose love, you will need no other reason to be happy.

> *"The only thing I take serious is life. It's all I have.*
> *It's all you have." – Anita*

As my father and I walked outside with my doll in tow, I looked back, feeling special and so very happy to be going home. This was the happiest time in my life as a child. Even though home was a dysfunctional war zone, I got to appreciate it for what it was. Even if it was bad, it was what God had given me, and from that, I picked up the pieces and created a life I could tolerate. It was time to let go.

I often wondered why God allowed me to live. I felt like one of his angelic disciples. We are all disciples. When little Julia died, I felt part of her spirit come into me. When I left, I looked back at that institution and felt I was leaving with a gift that wasn't material, but ethereal. I was both happy and sad. Most of all, I was glad to be me. While looking back, I saw all my hospital friends waving to me at the window. I might have been looking back but it wasn't about going back—but rather it was looking to where I was going. Even now in life, I don't go back. I just go wherever I'm going. This is the present moment—real time.

"I held my life higher than any negativity around me." – Anita

When we arrived at my house in Philadelphia, everything seemed so foreign. Instead of feeling home, I felt distant. There were at least 50 kids milling about with presents for me. I felt like royalty—like Princess Grace of Monaco on a prodigal trip back to her homeland of America, which, in this case, was Philadelphia. The kids were all screaming when the car pulled up. Then silence descended like a veil over everyone as my father opened the door and I stepped out. The silence was golden. This was one of those special moments that seemed frozen in time. I learned about the tremendous, quality aspect of time in those precious, suspended seconds. I understood that bonding would be different with these kids even more so now than in the past. Perhaps they had learned something about themselves and how precious life is because of my ordeal. That moment was an artist's delight. I could capture it, hold to it—but I couldn't bottle it.

All I could see was the light when I got out of the car—the light and joy of my renewed life. That was a sacred moment. You could have heard a pin drop when I got out of the car. I felt as high in rank as the Pope—as high as the Goddesses Hera, Tara and Durga. My spirit glowed with awe and wonder even as young as I was. I felt like I had risen from the dead which, in reality, I had. The other children looked at me and sensed that I was different. After a solid five or ten minutes of silence, they came to me one by one and handed me a gift. That overall feeling has and will continue to stay with me forever. Every day is my birthday and I celebrate my life. This is the inspiration I bring to everyone. What are you celebrating?

I became an advocate for health and fitness, representing people with heart conditions. I felt I had a healthy heart because I lived and I wanted other people to have that too. I even raised the most money in one year for the AHA in my district, and received a promotion letter in the mail. From there I took off with it. I knocked on every neighbor's door and refused to leave until they dug into their pockets.

"I saw the meaning of life at age nine.
It takes a lifetime for some to come to this." – Anita

Philosophies & Lessons From Chapter 3

Philosophies
"Living on the edge & opening my heart to my higher self." – Anita

That's what it was like in the hospital and is that way in life. Experiencing life and the unknown; how much to give—to receive, knowing where and when to take action, knowing how much energy to release and how much to retain was all a delicate balance. This balance became the middle and I became the pendulum. I functioned between the edge and my soul. This is how I learned to be me. Somewhere along the way, I found love and learned to shift from life to the edge. When on the edge, I needed to survive, but the edge widened and became life without boundaries, without structure and without hierarchies. That is where I flourished.

Love is an art. I used my body and created from the thoughts and feelings that came from within, the beauty of expression. I opened up to people. I laid bare my heart to the human race. That very opening is probably what healed my heart. I felt special; I made a guru out of myself, wanting to share my gifts with the world. That is liberation and enlightenment.

I relate to pop singer, Madonna, because I believe she opens her heart to the whole human race. She wrote a song called, *Open Your Heart.* The fact that she opens her heart and liberates her thoughts is why she is successful. That is sensual. We can all be successfully sensual if we become inclusive.

"Opening my heart to the human race." – Anita

When we play the edge, we expand our shifts. The edge is going to the end and being able to find balance—from there creating a reservoir from which to move. Some people live too much on the edge and end up staying there. The key is to be able to recognize the edge as a risk and a challenge. The edge teaches us our limitations and progressions. The edge is that place before the pain—before the breakthrough—before we ride the moment. We must experience the edge before allowing it to be. We need the edge to stimulate our consciousness and internal growth. Playing the edge is an awareness of working within the limits. Encountering our edge helps us to see straight ahead to the place we want to be. You experience conflict by resisting who you are and who you can be. Encountering the edge is breaking away from the old, false patterns that were once created by the energy of others. The key is to be aware of your own energy and know your space.

The idea is the ability to give in to your edge and move forward with the changes. When we hover into our edge, we are preparing for whatever lies ahead. Staying in the moment is the edge. You need to be able to take it out or take it back. It's the energy that you learn to direct— the push and pull. Move forward when you're ready to open. Staying where you are is equally as important. The goal is to contain our edge, to know where it begins and ends as well as how to approach it without fear and pain. Your body is the vehicle to get you there.

Overstretching when you're not ready is about wanting to meet those unmet goals and needs. When we meet the edge, we discover our newness and from that point, real life begins. This is your depth—your truth. The edge teaches us the difference between being assertive and attentive.

"Loneliness can be a gift." -Anita

I felt extremely lonely when I entered the hospital when I was just nine years old, knowing that I would be there for many months. But there's a soft place in your heart that sometimes talks to you. If you listen to it and open yourself to it, you will realize there is no such thing as *loneliness*. When we are depressed or are coming out of a relationship, we say we are "lonely." That feeling is conveyed by a need for self discovery. Loneliness can be a gift—the opportunity for you to look deeper into yourself.

However, the terms; *"loneliness," "being a loner"* and *"being alone"* are all different in meaning. Loneliness stems from a sense of emotional neediness and is usually temporary; being a loner means you are more comfortable with yourself; and being alone is the acceptance of your own company and is a choice. If you spent a lot of time alone in your childhood, you may understand this. If we feel unsatisfied, we can move away from our suppression using the body, thereby placing ourselves in the middle of life and reconnecting to the human race. Next, trust develops and we can become authentic—the real us.

It's about "being in the alone." Can you find that part of yourself? I love being alone today. I'm not lonely, but I am a loner and yet I have many friends. In fact, I'm usually considered the 'life of the party.' I'm like a chameleon because I am able to live different eclectic parts of my full self, expressing my full potential. All of these parts are the "real" me. We need to learn early on to strengthen our emotions because life only gets harder. I had to connect with me first. That made it easier for me to connect with others. I worked hard to build the "Power of Love" in myself and you can too.

"The heart has a different language than the mind." – Anita

Throughout history, our most esteemed poets believed the heart is the executor of our emotions. Unlike other muscles in the body, the heart is an involuntary muscle. It beats and moves on its own. Its function is to circulate blood throughout the body, to nourish the other organs, tissues and nerves. As it nourishes physically, so it nourishes emotionally. The heart needs to be trained, meaning, the heart gets confused sometimes even when, deep inside, we know the truth.

Since the heart has a life of its own, teach each other how to bring it out in our personalities. The emotional responses of the heart are modulated by internal stimuli, by experiences the mind and body have at any given moment. Anxiety begins in the heart. The heart beats faster when we are in certain stressful situations and, when that passes then it calms down.

We can convince our autonomic nervous system and heart to adapt to environmental changes. We can train our muscles and emotions to adapt to each other. The heart is a muscle but it is also the seat of our emotions. The heart has its own emotional life. Medically speaking, the heart is a delicate organ and requires exercise. The heart either overworks, underworks, or pumps inadequately to meet the body's needs. What the body needs, the mind also needs. When we are nervous, the heart beats with fear and anger—rapidly. When we are in love, it beats with excitement—staccato.

Since my time in the hospital, I've lived "in the mood," like the Glenn Miller song of the Big Band Era. I lived my moods to their fullest, because this helped me to be "real." I accepted every mood and didn't fight against myself or my will. I chose to identify through myself.

"Empathy was part of opening my heart." – Anita

I didn't have anyone to turn to with whom I could talk to about all I had been through when I was nine. Ironically, I understood the pain of my hospital mates when most of white America didn't. Those kids were picking on the wrong person. I was closer to being one of them rather than separate from them. That was just another transformation for me. I learned about empathy. I experienced the feeling in my heart for every person, realizing this was the path to getting well. I was still a child, so I hadn't been conditioned with a lot of hate at that point. I was able to empathize with the black children.

Today, I still feel the pain of other, but I am able to separate and transform in the moment, naturally sending out healing energy to that person. I empathized using the love I allowed into my heart. In every person, whether scorned or innocent, I am able to see the pure heart and soul residing in them simply, from my own heart.

Lessons Learned

The hospital experience taught me to never take advantage of other's emotions by ridiculing them. Every hurtful thing you say that is aimed toward another is "shutting-out" the inner expression of the self. Every time I felt afraid, I reached in and pulled out my "little girl" for strength. Prayer and Faith were my answers while I lay in my sweat, burning with fevers.

Gabrielle Roth, the movement guru, said to *"sweat your prayers."* Well, believe me—I did sweat my prayers literally during my red-hot burning fevers. Partly, due to the other children, I found out who I was. I was no longer a child, but an adult in a child's body. I had changed. Now, I knew who I was.

I learned from very early in the hospital to forgive myself. Then it became second nature.

> *"Remember to love yourself today and love someone else."*
> *– Anita*

CHAPTER 4

Excelling Through Love

"The life is the relationship because we witness each other in space on Earth." – Anita

Space is wonderful to have. Enough of it makes it a wonderful place to be. A little extra room is, at times, the best gift you can give yourself and someone else. This comfortable, invisible cushion is one of the most objective forms in human nature and is both within and outside of you. Space also serves as a barrier and an open form of matter. It is only an illusory opening that we feel is real. But, without this 'magic bubble,' we couldn't exist, because space is the empty plane from which we move in and out. It's the end of where we're comfortable and the beginning of where we are.

Within our bodies, we need space in order to function properly. Personal space is important for our humanity, sanity, relationships, and our existence—the space in the body—the openness around the body.

This invisible barrier acts as the medium between two people— between two objects. It's an empty illusion, something we don't see or feel yet, are present in. The vast emptiness, time and force combine to become the language of movement. If you've ever watched ballet dancers performing their graceful dances, you cannot deny that movement has its own language. Since space comes in all sizes, it has both a direction and an indirection. Some people are direct and blunt. Others are indirect. The latter tends to work around things while the former is straight to the point.

Time has its own rhythm. Force can be strong or weak and comes from within. It's concentrated energy. Simply said, we can be forced emotionally into a situation, or we can choose to be in that situation, supported by our invisible cushion. When overbearing people force themselves on you, they invade what was comfortable, your 'bubble.' That emptiness is vital to both emotional health and successful relationships. It's the middle and the "in-between." It's the silent, empty, open-wide place. This invisible barrier supports relationships, sounds, actions, and breath, while helping us clarify and define the true nature of our being. Like a glass of water, it's full, then empty after consumed.

In Kinepathics, we relate from the openness within the body. The body needs this space for longevity. Our organs need to share it. Space is a central force and is where our energy comes from—the more space in the body—the more flow and energy.

This empty, but vital area creates freedom and extends life. When we have it, we let go of unnecessary boundaries. Begin by focusing your energy on the open, empty spaces around you. This creates a relationship with gravity, and this is how you "feel" you're in the bubble around you. Space begins in the "inner self," then the outer, open space and the "relational space," or in-between.

This emptiness is just as important as the objects around us. While in the comfortable openness we create for ourselves, we breathe, eat, function, live and die. When we utilize space wisely, we realize our boundaries, our separations and we become centered. We balance and shift more easily when we are in the actual moment. Space allows us an awareness of the "silence within." It is in our being, the invisible boundary between you and your lover. This "stillness" allows the body to sustain and calmness. Then we go from being symmetrical and unyielding, to opening up just a little by incorporating a few body motions. This is so that the body knows when and how to take steps energetically. Then we "take it out" in full swing, becoming asymmetrical. All of this allows us to realize what "space action" is all about—how space provides so much in life. Most people take advantage of this comfortable barrier. They fill it with junk. Being aware of our space keeps us aware of whom we are while teaching us to use it wisely.

People often park, wasting spots that others could use. It makes you want to yell at them; "get out of my space." A lot of people are unaware of other's physical and mental boundaries. One of the keys to a healthy relationship is an understanding of the importance of this crucial emptiness. Couples are unaware of the need for openness around us—that it is an integral part of the relationship. There is a tendency to invade the space of others we are comfortable with too often, resulting in break ups or divorce. We must cherish our space and other people's as well. Being overly affectionate irritates one's mental barriers. When we have this extra room around us, we are comfortable with the identity of who we are, so we need this to maintain our being. We can then live and let live, letting go of any leashes. Couples, who divorce, lack the understanding of personal space. When you learn to maintain these invisible barriers while being with one another, you will always enjoy your feeling of independence and freedom, thus avoiding conflict. It's healthy to get away from each other for weekends at a time. Create an invisible barrier in your present environment and by separating once in a while.

When we learn to maintain the emptiness among each other, the feelings of independence and freedom soars. You can still have your identity even when committed to your body, your mate, your relationships. Allowing space for you involves structure, form, and freedom.

Within the openness, is the lovely factor known as time. It is the here and now that is happening. When life happens, it is but a fleeting moment then, it's gone. This is what each situation presents with a complex nature of the involved self. To let the soul be involved is a reality that we must face with each experience. I connected time to my soul and the time I have left on Earth. Time is precious. It is a part of sequential fitness. Time is the rhythmic response of an emotion.

My Story Continued
"It was the darkness of my soul, the blackness of my soul that became enlightened" – Anita

My grade school and high school years were challenging since, I had not only missed a year of the fourth grade, but the kids in school looked at me differently. Now I knew how black people felt. I found myself on the outer circle looking in most of the time. It was hard for the other kids to accept me. To them, I was different. The patterns of personal ridicule repeated over and over for years, so that it began playing in my head like a broken record. All the hate was coming from the world at large, so I stayed firmly connected to the love inside my heart. My soul would replenish in front of their faces. They couldn't relate to me. All they saw was the light shining from the God in me and that was fear to them. I had nowhere to turn again, but in.

Being home again was disturbing. Dad was always pushing mom around, not to mention having to manage my schizophrenic brother. I cared for my desperately abused mom and my siblings. I ended up raising myself and my brothers and sister. I just took charge. That's what we're supposed to do—stop complaining and take charge. Those kids looked up to me while teasing me at the same time. My mother was too weak from years of abuse. Every day, life for my family was like watching a drama on television. An excellent analogy would be like the movie, *Who's Afraid of Virginia Wolfe*.

When my parents fought, I would escape to the sanctuary of my room to dance in the mirror. This was the "secret" to escaping this painful part of my life. I created an isolated space in me. We are all looking for the secret, (relief), but the secret is within you. Your secret is whatever you find to relieve the victimization. It's how you find your balance. Even with the pain, I managed to keep a vision of laughter and relaxation.

People would put me down for any manner of ridiculous reasons. They put me down because of my sun sign, Scorpio, because of my long blonde hair, because of my Italian heritage, because of the clothes I wore etc. People often put down others in an attempt to elevate themselves beyond their own insecurities and self degradation. They were spiritually deficient. So, I learned patience.

I was the anger release doll for them. Today, I honor my anger. My mom taught me about emotional expression, feeling and anger when she performed her rituals of screaming high and low right there in our living room and when she sung her beautiful songs. At other times, I would stay in my bedroom with my hospital doll. "Aloneness" was my friend. My doll was a symbol of great worth to me.

As I have mentioned, one of my brothers was Schizophrenic; the other one was partially blind. He went to a special school for the deaf and blind. Our house was always full of many different types of kids. Children from the blind school visited often and my emotionally challenged brother was always there. We would often attend psychiatric meetings and therapy for my older brother. I was able to learn the Braille system with the other kids who were blind, and some sign language from those who were deaf and/or mute. The blind kids also taught me about sensory perception— *the non-verbal communication was very powerful and in the undulation is where I found a place without words.* I knew that existed in the body.

I had a lot of responsibility as a child, having to help rear my siblings as well as be a father figure to them, not to mention being the emotional "husband" to my mother. I learned to accept things as they were when I was very young. Like the Chinese Taoists, I learned to be happy with what I had in order to accept and embrace life.

"There's a whole world out there just waiting for you." – Anita

The Mummers
(Don't rain on my parade.)

The Mummers parade, a Philadelphia tradition, played a big part in my ability to open my heart to others. It has a history dating back to the late 1800's and is the most unusual, authentic and original parade I've ever seen. My father would have us camped out on the benches he designated every year at 7am. The Mummers are something you become while watching it. A lot of work goes into the creation of costumes and colorful floats, all for just one day. When you think about it, one day is what life is really about, isn't it? That and the choices you make.

The parade began among families and continues, today, to pass down through family members. It's a rich tradition of family and connection. Philadelphia truly is a family city, but with times changing as they are, the people and the city have made some drastic shifts, but the parade still goes on.

The parade comes once a year on New Year's Day. It's an event similar to Mardi gras, Carnival Rio, and Carnivale Italy all rolled into one. There are elements of "burning man" which takes place in the Black Rock Desert in Nevada every Labor Day. The mummers do their strut right in the middle of the crowded streets of Philly. It's an expressive strut —one to admire, to cry, to love, and to open up to others. It's a strut with attitude, purpose, direction, courage, meaning—a place to go and find the depth within yourself. This strut continues annually in the city of brotherly love.

The parade is a ritual created for healing and is a big part of the Philadelphian tradition. The comedic mimic clowns would kiss us as they strutted by. I learned to strut and gesture a new way every year. Women had never been allowed in the parade until as recently as the late 90's. The parade offers comics, fancy brigades, fancies and string bands, showering lots of Philly love born and freed from its suppression on this day each year. I think every city should have a traditional, yearly parade like the Rose Bowl in Los Angeles, the Mummers in Philadelphia, and the Macy's Thanksgiving Day parade in New York. The mummers helped me celebrate my life. If it weren't for them, life would have been exceedingly dull. Thank you mummers with all my heart.

"When we have passion, everything is easy." – Anita
"I celebrate the life my parents gave me everyday" – Anita

Free Me

When my parents fought, I would cry to myself and wish that my life was different. I would punch the wall in anger and frustration. Abusive families make kids more aware of volatile emotions. I would walk and cry, pull my hair, hit the walls and ask; "Why? Why is my life so horrible? Why am I not fortunate enough to be from a normal family?"

Parents need to learn, understand and be aware of what their kids are expressing behind closed doors. Where was one to go, but inward? I could only exchange the hate by transforming it to love again. Life at home was so terrifying, that I couldn't wait to grow up and get out. *I got out mentally.* Yes, that's what you want to do. Get out mentally. Once you get out, you can run for freedom. You can now experience this part of yourself that you've never known. You can still be physically present in the lives of your family members and even be living nearby. Getting out mentally does not necessarily mean physically. Once you are out mentally you can look at them objectively and maintain your identity and then re-create your being. You can help them see the light.

Although, I learned to shift and escape mentally, I was still very much part of the ongoing education of my family. Because my life was so full of emotional baggage, I've taken the journey for my family. I have lived my mother's life. With all the hate I received from the outside world, there was much more love than I could imagine within myself.

A client friend of mine, Andy Hartnett, would often say "free me" meaning, he wanted out of his pain. Hopefully Andy is free now.

My experience with heart disease turned out to be a blessing in disguise. It helped me create and generate love. What else is heart disease, but a closing off of the heart chakra? *I taught myself to let go of the pain, let go of the negativity.* I, literally watched my little-girl-hood pass me by, but today she is alive and free. My spirit needed to love, live and be free. The pain of my family and friends' transferred into my energy. The ridicule I received from friends sometimes made me feel like *The Elephant Man.* I was labeled and hated. I was called names such as "pimple face." I grew up in the city of brotherly love, nearly drowning in a pool of hate. It's a wonder I took up swimming.

Labeling others is a way of neglecting ourselves. I wanted to become a nun, because I thought that was where I would find God. However, the more I loved myself, the closer I became to God. I wanted to be a boy, because it appeared they had much more freedom than women. However, in actuality, women are more emotionally free, so I haven't any envy over our male counterparts.

"I cherish life so much!" – Anita

I Dance Alone

When chaos invaded my sanctuary, I felt as if I were in the ocean, treading water, trying to keep myself from drowning. So, "living in my room" became the atmosphere of my life. To hold to my faith, I created a sacred space in my room. My fears eventually sent me into hiding, but I had my sanctuary. I was hiding from the precarious ghosts of my life, fading into a ghost myself. My feelings turned to shame which buried my soul, putting out my light. When I would dance in front of the mirrors, I would take joy in watching my every movement.

What I saw in the mirrors, literally taught me to copy the behavior of positive people. Every day, after school, I danced before my bedroom mirror. It seemed like I danced forever there. This became a regular ritual for me. It was my secret—"the secretive dance." I danced my secrets, my joys and sorrows. I would honor my bed before lying in it. I played music and worshiped myself in the mirror. I became wild and silly.

There were times when I paced around the house, milling in circles due to all the tension. My mother would encourage me by saying, "Listen to your body", that is how you'll know your mind.

I practiced the movements and gestures of others while I danced. I learned to love myself by dancing in the mirrors. My impulses connected to my emotions.

Madonna sang a song about coming home and dancing alone behind closed doors in the mirror.

"Heal yourself in the moment of abuse—
use that as a transformative tool... I did." – Anita

The Wilderness of Mirrors

It's okay to look in the mirror. It's okay not to be modest. Looking in the mirror can give you a sense of knowing where you are and how you get back to the world. It's like being an actor. You play yourself having to take on the role of being the "real you." Look in the mirror and practice gazing into your eyes. Kinepathics teaches you to honor the mirror and learn to praise yourself. Mirrors can help us build our identity.

When I was a teenager, I used to watch myself in the mirror, dancing and stretching. I used the mirror as if it was a person looking back at me. The mirror became my friend and, as a result, I was able to love and accept myself. I talked to it and, in my imagination, it answered me back. The mirror can be a positive force. The mirror is your friend. All I did was dance, stretch, and move in front of the mirrors in my room during family conflict. It was my hiding place, my refuge—my sanctuary.

"When we learn, we change, so if you want someone to change,
begin by teaching them." – Anita

I still remember when I was in the ninth grade. I had this algebra teacher named Mrs. Grubbs. She was from down south. The students made fun of her southern drawl so much that it's a wonder she stayed. I formed a mental connection with her and we shared the same moments in life. I empathized with her, and she with me. I knew what she felt but I couldn't stop the kids. I'll never forget her face and how alone she felt. This was a moment in my journey that I won't forget. She, too, was the target of ridicule. It was like she was trapped in a rainbow. I felt her pain. If only I had the strength at that time to stand up to and put the other students in their place. This made me think back to my tutor in the hospital who abused me and how I couldn't do anything about it. It caused a separation in me. Part of me wanted to be accepted by the students and be part of the group and the other part empathized, wanting to save the teacher from the "jungle." I took charge, stepped out and did what I wanted to do. I didn't care what the students thought of me. *I was liberating my feelings, thus connecting to my emotions, keeping them alive.* This is what people admire about me now. I went against the odds. I looked at her one day and experienced this amazing, true connection from my depths. *This was my first deep, connective, memorable experience with another human being.* I had waited so long for this. I was very much in the "present moment" with her.

> **"My biggest step to recovery was my relationship to my feelings."**
> *– Anita*

I didn't want to contribute to the fire with the other kids. Projection keeps us from truly knowing the wealth inside one another. I would approach her after class, because I wanted to be close to her—close to that familiar feeling of being hurt, a feeling that was normal for me. I never wanted to forget those feelings in my growth to this point. It was important that I revisit them so I could continually renew my senses. Mrs. Grubbs and I nourished each other's pain and vulnerability. I saw myself in her and this helped me love again. Because I empathized, I was healing. Mrs. Grubbs became more than just my algebra mentor. Math, being my most challenging subject, improved with the healing that she and I shared —so much so that I prevailed in algebra. I ended up with the highest score in the school—a total score of 100 all the way through. Then I realized that all it takes is love and you can learn anything. *Love is the power.*

With the attention-deficit/hyperactivity disorder (ADHD) I experienced, being attentive was challenging for me, but with love and compassion, it was as if I didn't even have the disorder. Mrs. Grubbs and I treated each other as the people we were. I never wanted ninth grade to end. This was but one special relationship that I'll always remember.

That experience was an opportunity to receive and give love and respect; something I so desired and needed. We can all find the missing links with a little bit of creative thinking. As a result of emotional intelligence, my intuitive processes strengthened. When we ridicule and project negatively toward another, we are stealing. It is a small, but violent crime.

Later, when I entered the tenth grade, a new experience washed over me. I, along with a faculty member, opened a group called "Reach a Person," or RAP. I was instrumental in receiving grants to help in the movement against drugs. It was rewarding for me to know that I was helping kids get off drugs while preventing others from starting.

I still didn't have any friends. I was finding my life's purpose, right there in those moments. We were a group termed "the students concerned with public health." It was during this time that I had another empathic experience. This time it was with my biology teacher. She was using drugs, but no one knew it, except me. I was able to break through her barriers and became an inspiration to her. We were required to do a project, so I did mine on drugs. I researched every drug there was and wrote about it. I still remember when I presented it. I stared my teacher right in the eyes with my inner power because, I was teaching her how dangerous the drugs were that she was poisoning herself with. She understood and I even recognized fear and other emotions in her. She didn't know who I was. I was her messenger. We are all messengers, we just have to be open to receive the message. That was another milestone moment in my life. I showed compassion and passion all in one moment. That was just the basic truth of intelligence.

I became involved in every activity possible, from chorus to theatre. I was so involved in the activities in life, that I received an award for four years of perfect attendance in high school. I had the willpower and the discipline of a yogi by this time from my CHH experience.

When I was in eleventh grade, I performed a pantomime piece titled *Dizzy Miss Lizzy* by Larry Williams. Both my mom and dad were instrumental in helping me with this. Mom taught me the dance steps and blocked me through the skit and my father made the wooden guitar for me. He painted it and made it look really good. Mom made my costume. Both of my parents put a lot of love into the preparation for this performance. I received a standing ovation from at least 600 high school girls. It was another tremendous moment I'll never forget. I was the talk of the entire eleventh grade year. My performance was unique and original. I jumped, sang and danced like I was dizzy. *Dizzy Miss Lizzy* was a very liberating experience for me as well as the other students. It was a shocking cutting edge performance at the time. I just did what I wanted to do; and so can you.

Sometimes I get labeled as the "dizzy blonde," but in all honesty, I open up to my wildness, my primal spirit, and allow myself to be who I am. This is how you let go of the suffering. Yes! Yes! Let go!

"Abuse can be turned into love, the greatness and the hurtfulness and the harm." – Anita

Life meant death for me. This is what life is about for every turning point that we experience. The pain of infliction, the internal cries, the entrapment all led to the development—the love of others, and encouragement—the behavior of eclectic empowerment. I believe that any attempt is the first step to recovery. Helping others became a hobby. I sometimes wished that the other kids could have been more like me. People didn't understand what they feared in me. Knowing better today, I believe they feared my "presence." Years of suppression inhibited my desires. My biggest effort is in connecting with people.

"When I connect, I find out a little more about myself." – Anita

X-Raying the Bones / Moving the Bones

After high school, I studied x-ray technology and worked 15 years in the field. Radiology was all about "breathe, don't breathe, hold your breath, move, don't move, move." For the second time in my life, I was the only white person again. My x-ray training program in 1974 was me and six African-American students who got along just fine. Society still hadn't come full circle with blacks and whites mingling.

There were two of us x-ray students, me and my white girlfriend, who had dropped out because that's what white people did if black people were present. Blacks still weren't accepted in society yet. America had succeeded in brain-washing her into believing that blacks and whites didn't belong together. I knew better. I knew we complemented each other in more ways than one. While white people were prejudiced against blacks, I was having dinner with their families; I was ahead of my time. They crowned me valedictorian of the class and I was honored and given the most outstanding student award. Just like the most outstanding patient award I received while in CHH, I knew there was something special about me. Others saw it.

People's bodies told their stories in x-rays. The movement that the body is capable of, the forward and backward bends describes the articulation of their space. I was drawn to the medical field after my own hospital experience. I definitely picked the right field in which to learn more about the body, breath, yoga and life. No one is aware that x-ray positions are very similar to yoga positions. It is when the body opens that we shoot a picture so doctors can evaluate possible diseases. For example; a back twist in yoga is an x-ray position that opens the spinal joints. A "bridge" (setu bandha) is sometimes used for certain pelvic x-rays.

X-ray was an unusual calling. It was a profession, a demand, a science, and an art. In fact, it's an art and science combined. Both the right and left brain are utilized at all times when performing an x-ray study. *"X-ray is a real art and, in some, an in-born talent."- Alleta Ojeda, Chief Technologist at Century City Hospital in Los Angeles.*

It took talent to get beautiful films or less than ideal body habitus and there's a talent in knowing how to view the work. X-ray technology encompasses every field. It's integrated artwork. I found x-ray to be rewarding in the sense that it employed the elements of photography, geometry, computer science, intuitiveness, psychology, architecture, fluid movement, and yoga. I worked with space, dimensions, layering, distance, and time. I also found that working in the darkroom was very meditative. I would spend at least two hours a day in the darkroom, developing films. Back then, we hand- developed them. This allowed me to find serenity and a sense of aloneness, thus harnessing my "presence"—slipping into the darkness of life on life. The darkroom gave me an unusual sense of being back in that hospital bed. I harnessed my aloneness. I was able to get away from the noise. I lived with a lot of darkness. Being in the dark encouraged me to search for the light. When in the darkroom, I was able to shut out the noise. Being around my black classmates, symbolized the difference between dark and light. I lived with a lot of inner noise and needed to find ways of getting rid of it. Between the hospital, the household and the elementary and high school students at school not accepting me and ridiculing me, there was a lot of other people's noise living in my head. I realized while taking x-rays, within the body was hidden, "the shadows of the truth."

"My illusion became my reality, my body is my art my illusion is my reality." – Anita

Finding Your Space

The body never lies. The story is revealed when it's unleashed. The more space in the body the more we connect to our expressive, instinctual nature. Our organs need room for the cells to live and function. It's about creating room and having a relationship to the space in the body and outside the body. This emptiness is developed when we first adjust our attitude toward life and become aware of our emotions toward ourselves and others. Space is the relationship the body longs for. The more space one has, the more life one has. It's about being the "real you." Learning to shift in and out of the boundary of your behavior is the nourishment that the body needs. The structure of the body is multi-dimensional. X-ray taught me that the body needs to move in and out of different positions and shapes in order for disease to flush from its hiding places out of the body, or at least not become a parasite to other organs, causing blockage.

It's no wonder that patients felt good after an x-ray. We positioned them and articulated their joints for an hour, until their bodies opened. I realized that the body holds the memories of all the years of our lives. All the trauma remains in the body. The body remembers its' time in the womb. All we did was move in the warm water. It's the primordial essence of love. Some x-rays involved having the patient breathe in and out while we shoot during each breath to catch the body part superimposed in motion. This breathing revealed a lot about the body to me. But something about catching an x-ray from the inside in motion as opposed to a photograph on the outside in motion intrigued me. Taking x-rays was like directing a silent movie. It taught me about the freedom within.

> *"It's the caring and compassion toward others that*
> *bring me happiness." – Anita*

After x-ray training, I went out into the world, working many x-ray jobs. It was at one such place that I met Mindy B. She showed me the peace that was to be found in swimming. It was her guidance that taught me about conserving energy through swimming. I began to swim at the hospital pool and found the exercise to be very fluid and peaceful. Now, I swim 3 times a week and never miss. Swimming represented to me the likeness of being in the womb again. It was a time of healing. Swimming became synonymous with the fluid and wave that had been living in my body since I was nine. I began 'undulating' my emotions under water. Swimming helped me sink into my deeper self. It was a place without words and helped me get away from all the surface noise. It was symbolic of life in the womb, of being in the uterine sack. Swimming allowed me to release endorphins and clear out any anger I felt.

I ended up getting two psychology degrees. My biggest psyche lesson was in the early home experiences of my life. X-ray training was a stepping stone for me. It served its purpose.

> *"The art of life is composure." – Anita*
> *" We learn by allowance and receiving" – Anita*

People who Self-Sabotage

It was other people's pain that abused me—their transference. Projection onto others is an avoidance of your own pain. Negativity is the weakness of others. This kind of treatment drove me to hate myself and lowered my self esteem, however I stayed on the path, determined not to lose myself.

The eyes are where we bond and connect. We sabotage ourselves every day. I became a victim of the gang's ridicule. People are conditioned to hurt others. It's the duty of a human being to protect each other's emotions. The oppressions of childhood, limited societal behavior and that's why the world is so dysfunctional. But, people live life like either a race car and skip moments, or they just keep managing to direct their lives instead of live in their lives, due to their limitations of thought.

The caged bird sings because he wants freedom. *Unexplored emotions in the body can lead to addictive behaviors.* Abandonment comes in many forms and can leave us always wanting more than we really need or deserve. Our pain is a cry for love. *Angry people need a hug.* Your body is the silent voice behind the opinion. Be a good person and enjoy your life. Be happy with who you are and what you have.

People used to sabotage me with their eyes. I carry "laughter energy." I've learned to laugh so much because of the pain. Laughter makes me whole, its comic relief. The phrase; "Laughter is the best medicine," is very true indeed.

"I've learned to love all that life offers because it's a pleasure."– Anita

Philosophies & Lessons From Chapter 4

Philosophies

When God gives us enlightenment, he means for us to carry on and spread the faith with courage. My faith drove me. If you lose faith, you lose life. To show faith is to be you. Rock singer, Bon-Jovi sings a song entitled *Keep the Faith.* God is in all of us, this is the divine. If we are ignorant to it, then we need to seek spiritual counseling. Prayer is the emotional transportation of the soul. I am God and we all are, but I feel my God. When we are "our real selves," we let God out. I often wonder why and how people can stay repressed for long periods of time. There's got to be something out there that triggers the soul and the mind to want to live. Hopefully the inspiration here. Wake up and create feeling within yourself and live. Sensuality is the feeling that you allow to be expressed. Each of us can become prone to enlightenment by way of development rapture. To live in your head is to bond with fantasy and unblock your imagination. The self of a person is so perfect and simple, yet so exploitive, inherent, fearful, alone, and rich. Eye contact is a form of support and gives us an anchor in the world. The heart speaks through the eyes, also known as the windows to our soul.

Most people don't know how to SET THEMSELVES FREE and "get

out mentally". I learned to do this as a result of opening my heart and loving myself. Love yourself and you'll be free. Then go back and teach your family. Somebody has to teach them.

We are coming to a time in life when it is necessary to teach each other more about life and love. Teach your parents how to love you—to forgive their past. Take the responsibility to teach your parents what they haven't learned yet and teach them what you need. Stop hating and forgive them as well as yourself for the world's sorrows. Take the power back with love. How else do you expect the world to get better? Starting over became a ritual for me. I am in constant renewal. You've heard the expression, "people don't change." Of course they do, they adjust and adapt. We are always changing, a little bit every day. Part of change is managing, growing and understanding your emotions. Change happens when we give ourselves the right to heal.

Feeling unaccepted is one of the worst feelings that I have experienced. I can relate to you and I want you to know that behind this feeling lies an ocean of love, and that when you show others that ocean, they can only transform a part of themselves into purity. It is YOU that must *liberate the moment.* I always felt special and yet different, a bit off-beat. Maybe you have felt that way from time to time. If you feel unaccepted, take a look in the mirror and honor your beauty and life. When you feel unaccepted, it's just that people haven't experienced what you have to offer yet. Therefore, they are unable to relate to you. So, go back in and honor your divinity. To feel unaccepted is to open up and keep going up that side that you developed and liberate it to the fools around you. Because if you don't, not only are you being treated like a fool, you turn into one. Being the fool is liberating and transforming. Loneliness is not a dead end; in fact it's a beginning. I felt that my gifts were crushed. All the fame in the world doesn't give me the joy of my gifts. It's the love inside that gives me back my joy, and yes, you can find it just as I did.

When we identify with freedom we have hit part of our truth. I resorted to my body temple for freedom and identified with nature—with life, with the present moment.

Lessons Learned

I learned lots of lessons along the way. It is possible to heal yourself right there in the middle of abuse. I became inspired by my life to write about it and am proud to have healed myself. From dark came light and the dualities were recognized.

I learned so much about the mind, movement and gesture and the conscious hidden voice in the senses. All of this life was painful but my mental notes are an inspiration to my own growth and, hopefully, to yours. I was able to separate my thoughts and let go of the suffering. I let go of each thing one by one and I did it myself with my own willpower. I learned that schizophrenia is nothing more than shut down Kundalini energy. Not knowing how to access this power of the Kundalini, keep parents taking their children to mental places where they suppress the symptoms with drugs.

I learned that intimacy is a big part of intelligence—"Emotional intelligence." I could learn anything quite thoroughly with this kind of connection. I later realized that because of the negative, I was surrounded with most of my life, learning was more challenging.

Living in my room taught me about the relationship to space, and me. Today I've learned not to judge life's pleasures such as eating and sex. I've learned not to put a lid on other's expressions. People say they hate food because it makes them fat and they hate sex because they've been hurt. To hate what's pleasurable in life is to fear death and death is any loss in life.

Trivia

I dance alone. To dance alone in the Zimbabwe, the Shona Culture (Africa,) is called Rufaro. Rufaro, or spiritual contentment, is achieved when one's basic needs have been met, leaving one free to care for others. A person with Rufaro is in a happy state of mind no matter how life treats him or her. During Rufaro, an artist captures this blissful state in a swirling dance of joy.

"Let the love in and feel it." – Anita

CHAPTER 5

❧

From Darkness to Enlightenment

" The power of dance; how I reclaimed my body"–Anita
"I only see the good in people" –Anita

The human body is the most powerful and beautiful of all art forms. Physical love is the most tender and compelling way of connecting with another human being, thus becoming a major force in life that exists in every person. Our sensual self must live. I believe the evolution of physical pleasure continues to blossom. For a moment, I want to revisit the feminine undulation of love and reveal its presence through emotion. A woman's body moves with the sea—an art form of its own.

When another person shows and feels an interest in us, we are attracting something from their past that connects with something from our past. We are connected solely by our spirits. Our relationship with our body is unavoidable. I have learned to appreciate myself as I am, while at the same time labeling myself. I have lived in and out of the body—this is a flexibility of the mind. Since the body, is mostly made up of fluids, it has a simile to the sea as a ship afloat in gear.

Whether or not you are aware of it, the body harbors your thoughts that are, later, expressed through motion. When people look in the mirror they can see themselves as being weak and dull. We see our false personalities. Then we make up our shapes and sounds to go with them. Others see a vast emptiness in the mirror. What do you see?

I used dance to heal the injustice that happened to me like Africans do, as my story continues in this chapter. I was able to work out my expressions while managing to keep a good head on my shoulders. This, of course, was risky business and one could be seriously hurt if they weren't careful.

There is an up and down side to everything. What I think it meant now, was that I was a part of the healing of Mother Nature. It is the essence of women that teach and heal the world. It was my way to let go of the suffering, because my body was suffering silently. I needed to express, be seen and move on.

Sometimes I would call myself the "ethical slut." After reading Dossie Easton and Catherine A. Liszt's book *The Ethical Slut*, it was okay. I never felt guilty. Neither did I feel like a slut. After all, the sexual revolution was alive. It was others that felt guilty—only because they weren't 'living'. We need to honor our sacred sensual self—our spirit. We need to honor ourselves no matter where we are in our lives.

My astrological sign is Scorpio, so I am ruled by the sexual region of the body. I was doing what my spirit drove me to do and the good thing was that I accepted it.

I was entertaining myself, dancing every beat and making history. Other people felt self important and ended up projecting negativity toward others, which they thought cleansed them of their impure thoughts and actions, when in reality, it created more hate in the world, even to causing their spouses to cheat. *The impurity is within the boundary of thought.* The feminine represents the embodiment of life.

We need to honor the feminine in us. Some women are inhibited, living out their masculine side just as men are masculine. When we smother our feminine, we are not honoring our deepest expression. Honoring the feminine in all of us is growth. When we don't grow, we become a parody of the self—dull. This is exactly why the world is in crisis—because the feminine is suffocating. Honor and rock your divine feminine.

As sleazy as radio jock, Howard Stern, comes across he is helping women honor that part of them in his own way. He makes the stripper feel good about what she does, who she is. He encourages it, making a star out of them. This is honoring the feminine, and it is why he's successful.

It is the man who honors the feminine in women that, by so doing, becomes successful. Stern helps women see that what they are doing is worthy, nothing to be guilty about and is ok to be who you are. . I used to dislike him because he labeled the woman, but now I admire what he does. It's all a matter of the way you look at things. Stern is liberating. In essence, women are not serving the man, but rather the feminine in all of us. I had a chance to visit his show a few times when I worked in radio. I felt like an object due to the whole stripping business and the men, but I held onto my power. It's the labels that keep us tied to the masculine, suppressing the natural feelings. Such labels suppress mother earth. The message here is to honor the sacred feminine.

We are living in a time when the world is in crisis and the feminine needs to come alive in all of us, both men and women. Now is the time for women to teach men to love and open up to their feminine nature. I believe we are on the verge of the evolution of a man's character, which will be measured not by the size of his manhood, but rather by his ability to love and be loved—by his vulnerability and receptivity. This would be a wonderful gift to the world. When nature is in chaos, the Mother divine which is in all of us is not being honored.

The goal of a woman, in today's society, is not to serve men but rather control them. When a man opens to his feminine nature, there will be no need for control. Giving up the sacred takes from the spirit, but Tantra yoga teaches us otherwise. I had to put myself in the fire to learn from the experience. Women are putting themselves out there and learning. This is why Tantra yoga is on the rise, so that we can teach more than just the physical act of love—we can teach how to cultivate the heart of love. This is grown from experience.

Again, it's about going back to the Mother earth and ourselves as the resource. Men are givers. It's when they are not in their feminine nature that they become takers. Deep down they know that, once the height of sexual pleasure has been achieved, their own power is fleeting. Camille Paglia states the fact that, "men fight a war that can't be won and western culture is the dazzling carnage that their havoc has wreaked."

"My emotions are like blood, they need to flow." – Anita

My Story Continued

For many people, sex becomes an abusive process of acting out with no identity. I danced through my raw, sexual feelings. To act out in a harsh, sensual way is a raping of the self. It's self sabotage that oppresses us all. This can lead to carnal addiction. It also leads to work that both men and women turn to that is nothing but the physical act. Sexual addiction is high on the lists among men and women today. When we use labels on our presence, we become lost.

"It's the stuff we are not dealing with that impact our mate." – Anita.

Rape. A Wake-up Call. A Time to Relearn

It was September of 1987. I was only 30—a time when I was getting comfortable with "being a woman." One night, when I was out with a boyfriend, I was drugged with drinks and date raped by him and six of his friends. I didn't ask for it, I didn't want it but there was nothing I could do about it. This is sick, perverse violence that men commit. Men still haven't come into their "presence" and time yet. *Love is the animal in you that we must connect to, so that we can run wild with the heart.*

Women, we need to teach and love them, not hate them for their ignorance in perpetrating this vileness. These men were college graduates, innocent of lawlessness, and came from good families.

I ask, "Why? What did this do for them?"

It was a condemnation of women, of the feminine—of something they were in denial from learning more about. They didn't have a clue. Essentially, most men want to be feminine. This is why they lust after the feminine with determination. Times have changed. Both men and women wear the feminine and masculine cloak today. The two polarities will eventually share the same sky. The newest trend is the "metro sexual" man. It's the war of the sexes, the countries, the races and so on that brings about these things; these acts of senseless violence.

When we are whole, our spirit is there to protect us, but they drugged me and then raped me. They fed me "screaming orgasm" drinks as they called it. A shutting down of the feminine voice. Men were, and still are, repressed emotionally because they lack feminine energy. If they aren't screaming inside to reach their feminine, then they are repressing their nature. Did this make them feel more powerful, more like a man? Who was the victim here? I was, for the moment—them for life—a victim.

I was searching, in the beginning stages of healing then; so, attracting the bad was easy. When we are not whole, we attract just that, the bad, the negative. It is important to work on our emotions every day in order to recognize who we are and to be able to love ourselves even more when we feel the need to be in the company of people that might hurt us.

I learned a lot about rape then; at first thinking that it wasn't rape because he was a boyfriend, then thinking that rape had to involve walking down the street and getting mugged. This opened up a whole new chapter in my life. I had to forgive myself, my womb experience, the heart hospital, and now the rape. As years droned on, I watched other women in rape counseling groups that I attended, and found that they didn't know how to forgive. Some gave up their rights to love again. I am proud to say that I was able to rise above this again with the help of the love that I have for myself. I love men and sex.

Why should I live with their pain and be a victim? Not all men are like that. (This was a profound awakening.) I learned how to get my power, my feminine and my soul all back where it belonged–to me.

For men, it is natural for the novelty of a woman to wear off. What is left but control and rape? I had thought that the low socio-economic class was more susceptible to rape. There is a good percentage that, unfortunately, goes unaccounted for. The college rapes are usually committed by rich men. Wealthy people think they can have everything because they have money and they know people in a higher chain of command. The guy who raped me was a rich boy from a very wealthy family. Well, no one gets out alive, no matter whom you know or what you have.

I learned that society takes a political approach with which to assign emotional value. Emotions are like the heart, they have an involuntary life. The body is just the shell that holds them together. The mind is the defense against the outside versus the inside world. This rape was another turning point in my growth. Subconsciously, I had to put myself through the experience to learn, understand and replenish my soul. We have control of everything that happens to us, so my advice is to grow from every event whether bad or good. I use my own experience as a tool for the teachings I present on sexuality. I use all my experiences to my advantage. We know our destiny.

I believe we all get raped when we sleep together when there is no intimate connection. Prostitutes, subconsciously, allow themselves to be raped again and again. Thank goodness for the undulations I learned when I was nine. They helped save my sexual life. The undulations were my movement of love, my way out of pain. Yes, I put up barriers and shut down, but with years of moving my pelvis, I made a full recovery. The rape was just another eventful trauma that played out one scene in the movie of my life.

Rape enlightened me and gave me more strength and wisdom. I realized that rape was a big result of not enough fatherly love. Because of that, I attracted all the wrong people, hoping for love. We attract what we emotionally experience. The predators are waiting. My advice is to reflect on your life, take charge of the losses, write each experience out, and work on healing each loss.

"People who project are in fear of their own spirit surfacing.
Reach out and love them." – Anita

The rape happened during a time when women were still in hiding over things like this. Where were the female politicians then? We need more females in politics if the world is going to survive.

It was hard to prove the rape. However, I did take the steps and brought it to the law. Lie detector tests were given to all seven men. This was a wake-up call for them and for me. Since it took place in a wealthy suburb of Philadelphia, the detectives claimed that women pull stunts like this because they are after money from men. The PCP drugs they gave me almost caused me to jump from a window. It had all the makings of a great CSI story. Where would those guys have been now? I hired a male attorney who actually went against me, working more on the male side of things. He practiced corruption. I had no one to turn to but my male friends. All the women, sisters, were against me because I was different.

We have come a long way. Women are all sisters these days. Because my sisters abandoned me, I turned to men and experienced rape in the inner recesses of my mind. I even reported my attorney to the bar because I believe he and the rapists worked together in an effort to save themselves by degrading women. Now, I understand why it is that I have become an emotional monster, taking life by the horns and why I have this masculine strength about me.

The movie *Monster,* starring Charlize Theron put it all together for me. Sit back and reflect on your monster, the dark side, and see if you could turn inward for a minute and forgive.

The city crimes unit sent me to a psychologist who was very insensitive to my feelings. She was very similar to the heart hospital tutor I had. This psychologist was unable to handle the hard core person that I had become, not only from the rape, but from my entire life to that point. I was unable to cry, to show how badly I was hurt by the rapists. She didn't know how to handle this defensive, walled behavior. My resiliency scared her. I was numb and resilient at the same time. It took years before I could deal with the walls I put up, so I turned to the x-rated world of strip dancing because dance was a way out of the body—a way of expression —a way out of pain.

Although strip dancing can create barriers, at the time it was opening and saving me. My life had been a rough one so far and I needed to get back to the wave, the fluidity. I believe that men rape because they fear their own feminine nature that waits to be awakened. Spiritual growth accelerates when one retains the semen. Learning how to function with this sacred sensual energy and directing it in the right way is healthy.

Men are inspired by feminine beauty. Women are an inspiration to the world. Rapists are so inspired, they rape. *The spiritual and sexual energy are one. Love is the freedom.* Men reclaim their bodies through women. I reclaimed by body through my dancing. Now is the time for the masculine, a time to re-examine its roots.

"Being a seeker is embracing ignorance." – Anita

Endometriosis

It was after the rape that I found I was afflicted with endometriosis. This is a disease that affects 5 million women worldwide. I believe it develops as a result of holding onto anger and fear. Women are trapped in their bodies when they have this disease, and it affects the mind. It occurs when the tissue that lines the uterus, called the endometrium, is found outside the uterus anywhere from the abdomen to the rectum. This misplaced tissue develops into growths or lesions that cause internal bleeding every month at the time of the menstrual cycle. The tissue builds up, breaks down and sheds. It results in a breakdown of blood and tissue from the lesions, inflammation, pain, infertility, adhesions, bowel, and sexual intimacy challenges, which can and often do occur. Endometriosis is being considered as a possible autoimmune disease since it emulates similar symptoms. It also affects the connective tissue throughout the body.

Sex can be very painful when you have endometriosis. This part of my body was shut down. Yes, it needed to be opened again. I believe that disease breeds in us because of the traumas we experience. I prevailed over this condition. I let go of the pain from the rape and the pain of the womb so that I could have sex again like any other normal person. I accomplished this through the undulations and the breathing exercises.

Lots of women with endometriosis experience a less than ideal sex life due to the pain. Not to mention, the bleeding lasts anywhere from 7 to 10 days. The clotting and internal bleeding is so bad that diapers are the answer, forget about tampons if you have this. I hold support groups and am the Los Angeles group facilitator. If you are living with endometriosis, I encourage you to visit this website. www.endometriosisassn.org.

"Liberation is freedom within structure." – Anita

Pope John Paul II

Wherever there is dark there is light. Right after I had been raped, I took a trip to the Vatican City. I wanted to find my worth again, my sacredness that had been robbed of me with that one act of violence. I did not know where to go or who to turn to. India hadn't been on my list of events then, so I went to Rome.

I made my way to a Papal audience which occurs every week. I had been on a bus tour with some people that I didn't know. I remember there was a woman I had a conflict with throughout the trip. During the Papal audience, I made sure that I was in the front where they had roped it off. The Pope walked around and only shook hands with those in the front. I had this need to get close to him—to touch him. I needed to see and feel his presence in me so that I could heal.

Out of the 5000 people that regularly visit on papal visit days, the Pope only shakes about 100 hands and I was one of them. I wanted to become free from my pain, sorrows, mistakes and the impurities from the rape. I asked God to "free me!" from the evils that lived in my body.

Suddenly, I felt like God reached out and grabbed me, similarly to when I left the heart hospital. Most people took his one hand and kissed his ring. I took both his hands and held them tightly and all I could see was his spirit. He was this white spirit that filled the space right there in front of my eyes. It was a real spirit to spirit connection. The Pope experience made me realize that God is in all of us and that we need to look to each other for higher power connections to our deeper self.

In life, we look to connect spirit to spirit and soul to soul, but it takes a lifetime to understand it. That's why we are here lifetime after lifetime, to clean and refine the spirit so the soul can live on and healthy new souls are born. I was only 30 when I realized the true spirit did exist in human life. This wondrous experience with the Pope was just another message from God that it's okay to be who you are because we are all spirits. Spirit has a hard time living in the human vessel; it's a constant fight between the rock and the hard place. When we resist growth and newness we are in fight with the spirit.

When I went outside, everyone was touching me, hoping to get a "piece of the spirit." The woman I had the conflict with, also had the good fortune of touching the Pope. She and I came together and embraced each other with love. There never really was a conflict—it was just an illusion infringing on our senses. This is how I know that love makes it all okay; like I knew with the kids in the heart hospital. It was that same feeling.

After the papal experience, I found that my spirit was renewed again. I had regained the purity that I had come for. I was sent there.

Pope John Paul II was more special than most since they made a saint out of him—a high priest ordained by God. The sacredness of my soul and feminine energy was born again at that moment while I was touching the Pope's hands. This was Shaktipat for me. The Pope, as well as Hindu deities and high priests of other cultural traditions, have this special gift of shining the spirit back on us—if we are open to receive it.

To receive, we must be in the "present" moment. Any Pope is a high priest, but sometimes people don't see them as such because they are part of the religious political circle. I have been a student of God since the womb and heart hospital days. It is my journey to continue.

> *"I relied on the spirit in bad times to grab me and heal me*
> *and boy did it. I am a miracle." – Anita*

The point I am making is, when you happen to cross paths with people, reach out and love someone who is spiritually insufficient— one who is venting and projecting—because underneath the negativity, lies a cry for help. These people don't know how to love and so they are in pain. I am able to recognize this in people and have had many experiences with people who have projected their insufficiencies on me. Sadly, they push away the pure spirit when it could have healed them, giving them joy. Please reach out and love others. By doing so, you are also, loving yourself.

> *"Celebrate life while you got it instead of complaining."– Anita*

Bali, Indonesia

One other place of note while on my journey to enlightenment was Bali, Indonesia. Most of my time there was spent in Ubud. I spent an entire month there trailing through the most incredible Hindu temples. The Balinese were very friendly and are devout in their beliefs. While I was there, I had the occasion to witness a "cremation ceremony." This consisted of a parade that ran the course of an entire day. Hinduism, Jainism and Buddhism all mandate open air cremation. The body is seen merely as an instrument that is used to carry the soul.

The Bhagavad Gita quotes, *"Just as old clothes are cast off and new ones taken, the soul leaves the body after death to take a new one."* The dead body is not sacred once the soul leaves it. In Sikhism, burial is not prohibited, although cremation is the preferred option for cultural reasons, rather than religious. Sikhs and Hindus both scatter the ashes in holy rivers.

Hindus prefer to destroy the corpse by fire rather than burying it in the ground. They do this to induce a feeling of detachment in the freshly-disembodied spirits, which is helpful in encouraging their movement into the other world. During last rites, a Puja ceremony is performed. Puja is a ritual worship ceremony. Unlike India, Hindu cremations in Bali resemble a community carnival complete with a parade that features marching gamelan bands and high spirits, which attract many tourists. People camp out for this festive parade honoring the exiting of a soul from the body to the other world. Unlike our culture, death is a precious time for the Balinese and yet it is a revitalizing moment. Death is the beginning of life all over again. Cremation ceremonies are an occasion of great happiness, not mourning. The ceremony represents the liberation of the spirit so that their souls can attain a higher world and be free for reincarnation. They are guided by their spirits as we are our egos. This is not an everyday occasion but takes place every five years in Bali. People stay buried until this time and then they are cremated or the path to reincarnation is cut off. If families have the money, they can always have a private cremation without burial.

I also had the privilege to witness a 'metal ceremony.' This ceremony was a day to worship "metal." I saw people shining all their metal possessions such as cars, motorcycles and so on. This was followed by a parade as well.

Rigidity Equals Oppression
Resiliency Equals Freedom

Marvin Gaye sang about sexual healing. High ideals and a strong drive combined, formulates the purity of a woman. When a woman is guided by the voices of her soul, her strength is like armor. Joan of Arc was a perfect example of this. I always feel that it is inner purity that allows me to continually rejuvenate. I was a lost girl in a small world wondering how fast to take the turns. Then, rigidity set in. The loss of this cast me into what I call a "prehistoric match of sobriety." I was still a lonely girl. This entire experience of expression was a crucial body moment in my life. I never felt the expression, the physical and emotional were blatant and it was as if I was emotionally and physically dead. It lay in my body wanting to come out, to manifest itself in some other way.

This was one of many experiences to come that left me emotionally starved. It lay in my body and just crept up on me later. I was still alive. I only wished that I had someone to guide me then. All women in their thirties should be big sisters to the girls in their twenties.

Anger is a disease. When we judge others we avoid who we are. Expressing anger is a natural way of life. I recommend that we see through each other's anger instead of judging. Replace the anger with love. With a little love, people respond differently. The ability to see through another's emotions allows you to grow and explore your own qualities, thus, becoming more self-assured when dealing with people. Energy is only seen, felt, and heard through the experiences of humans during shifting. When our energy splits off, it causes a block between repression and expression.

"Feelings are neither right nor wrong." – Anita

I punished myself for years for being raped. Rape victims will generally punish themselves and, for years, I believed that it was my fault. Statistically, 80% of women who've been raped turn to some form of prostitution. The rape they experienced destroyed whatever good they felt about themselves, so they feel they have to play to a man's vulnerabilities and get a reward for it. By doing this, they feel that everything is okay. I believe that men hate women, if only on a subconscious level. On the same level, they may even hate their mothers.

"Feminism's main problem for the last twenty years has been that it is incapable of appreciating art." – Camille Paglia

When I Look in The Mirror I See my Presence

This was a time in my life when I went from looking at the insides of bodies through x-ray in work, to exposing my body in the x-rated sense of dance. Somehow they went back to back. Afterward, I began strip dancing for men. Gradually, I slipped into the dark side of life as society knows it. I saw those moments as healing moments. We are all dancers and exhibitionists to a point. Knowing that my body is my art and an expression of who I am, I decided to dance through my vortex of feelings. The only people that would watch were men, so I danced for them. They needed it. It was scary and shameful at first, but I was a goddess and, as such, belonged to everyone, or so I was told. Yes, I was labeled and objectified. The real shame I was living with was the rape. It was this shame that needed to live and express its essence. I was able to do it through the dance.

"The Divine in me honors the Divine in you." – Anita

From X-Rated to Jazzin' it Up

It was the soul in Jazz music that tied it altogether for me—the pain, the sorrow, the moments, the times, the heart, the distance, the separation, and the harmony.

Along my journey, I met George Van Horn, the owner of an electronics school in Philly. He had a small radio station and those were the first air waves from where my voice was heard. That was where I got my start. I began with a show called *Philly Happenings.* Then I went on to Temple University to study broadcast journalism. I played jazz music on air and wrote medical stories. I became a two-time, national award-winning medical journalist.

My favorite sanctuary, away from the outside, was when I was locked in the DJ booth at 3 am playing and listening to the pain behind the words of all the jazz greats. I enjoyed receiving calls from people who were up all night, commiserating their pains and sorrows, listening to how the music was part of their story. That was one of my favorite places during this part of my life.

I interviewed some of the jazz greats, went to their performances and, later, to their funerals. I still remember going to Dizzy Gillespie's funeral as well as writing the story about him. My favorite was jazz vocalist Abby Lincoln who lived the music, the word and the stage. I had the privilege of interviewing her twice.

As part of my explorations in journalism, I visited the Howard Stern Radio show a few times. When I visited the show it was purely an exploration in broadcast. The station I worked for fired me for going on his show and feeding into his frenzy of life, but it wasn't long before they took me back. Stern and I had our debates, but this is a whole other story, destined for another book.

Another positive moment during this time, for me, was in a woman named Nancy. She would call me every time I was on the air—like a secret admirer. Sometimes I felt like I knew her. Nancy would call me at 4 in the morning to tell me that she heard the pain in my voice when I talked. She heard it coming through. This brought tears to my eyes—the first that threatened for longer than I could remember. Nancy was my angel—my counselor. She was who God sent me. Nancy gave me lots of support over the phone. She was the "ear," the shoulder I could cry on that I had longed for, for way too long. It was her bright spirit that heard my voice, and my pain. She encouraged me to make the change and move to California.

I was a loner, my parents were emotionally gone, people that I thought were my friends, didn't accept me, but Nancy was heaven sent. She began to share her story with me of the traumas of being battered by her husband. She was working toward building a catering business. I remember that she sent me a brochure about it. Nancy's gratification for helping herself was when she was helping me. I wanted to help her escape the man who battered her, but the pain stayed right there with the Jazz music, in the dark of the night.

Nancy helped me with my emotional struggles, which helped me see life with greater clarity. I saw the miracle inside me and also in the moment. We both honored our pain. *The messengers are there, we just need to see them and hold onto them. This means sharpening your awareness day by day, getting to that level of consciousness that is rhythmic for you. It means listening to you—reading between the lines, and asking the question. What will you ask?*

"To love is to learn. The miracle is in the moment." – Anita

One other night on air, a black girl called and said she knew me. She knew my name and asked me if I had been a patient in the Children's Heart Hospital approximately 20 years ago. It shocked and surprised me that she remembered my name. I do remember that by the time I left CHH, the black kids and I were friends and had taken pictures of us together arm in arm. It all stopped there. We wrote each other for years after having truly made a connection. To think that she would be listening to jazz music in the middle of the night, when I was on the air, spinning the records as a way of hiding my pain was very special. It was all coming full circle. *It seemed like wherever I went and whatever I did, there were angels. The power is the God in you giving back to yourself. God will send what you need if only you ask.*

The music taught me about the different pains that people have, and the separation between the beats helped me connect with a new part of me. For every jazz song I played, I was able to identify with greater clarity, the depths of my soul. This was what, ultimately, brought me full circle.

Stephen H. was a man I met who confessed to me he was an alcoholic and asked me how he could get rich. I explained that getting rich is within one's own heart. When I interviewed jazz vocalist Abby Lincoln she quoted; *"We all have gifts, but when we celebrate them, we are rich. Abundance is in any form."* She was saying that you don't know what rich is until you celebrate and honor your gifts and if you don't, then you aren't anything special anyway. Having money is far from rich.

"Miracles are the things that God puts in front of us. We just have to notice them. We have to see with all of our senses." – Anita

From Philly to New York to California

After working x-ray for a while, I realized that I needed to explore other areas of life. I went into radio and public affairs then, went on to Temple University to study. I studied massage in order to keep connected to the body. At the time, my boyfriend, John Simon, was a jazz musician in New York. He encouraged me to move there. It was 1990 when I made the move to New York. When I got closer, our relationship grew further apart. It was, quite literally, too close for comfort. I was suffering again, needing to find a way inward. The way out of suffering, for me, was in my body, using undulations. This is what Kinepathics is all about. I was always searching because, wherever I turned, there was pain, suffering, and conflict—leading to loneliness. I felt I was too evolved over other people for them to understand my nature.

The next place I worked was as an intern at CBS. I was an assistant producer in the book department, world news and medical stories. I also worked part time taking x-rays at a nearby hospital. My continuous searching led me to a class on movement at HB, (Uta Hagens School), studios where I was fortunate to study with the legendary Mary Anthony. Before this, I had studied movement with Rennie Harris of puremovement in Philadelphia. It was after Mary Anthony's class that I knew I had found what lived in me since I was nine—the undulating wave motion that waited to be expressed.

I needed to find more teachers to help me further develop this. It was the real deal. I was so excited to find what I needed—the support to develop the undulations for the expression of emotions. I spent two years in

New York, then moved back to Philly to prepare for my move west. Los Angeles it was. My memories of CBS were that people were afraid to love; the business was cut-throat so no one could show compassion even if they wanted to.

The office politics there disrupted my biorhythms, but the movement class I had been taking, helped relieve the tension. So, I continued my journey to LA. I felt my calling to the Golden State. After my experiences with Marianne Williamson and Sondra Ray, I felt it was a clear indication of my true calling.

I had been visiting LA for years so it wasn't a culture shock to me. I did interviews at the Oscars one year for the television station in Philadelphia that I had been working for with RJ and Joe Vitale. I began in the acting business at first, which was a part of the calling. I continued to explore and found several movement and dance classes. I studied movement with Marianne Karou, Emily Conrad, Anna Halprin, Camille Maurine, Gabrielle Roth and many more. I became immersed in many spiritual studies, Reichian and bioenergetics therapies, contact improvisation and other breathing therapies, mime, theatre arts, yoga and tantra studies. I also became a student for every kind of yoga taught at every studio—from tantra Kundalini to ashtanga. My resume is about 50 pages from all the workshops I have attended. It is how I came to develop Kinepathics Method of Life Solutions.

"If you connect to the spirit, you never have to die." – Anita

When I dance, I become sensual and I feel my sexuality. It becomes one with me—with who I am. Sensuality is not sex, but merely another way to your expression. The physical act is a part of my body, while sensuality is a part of the spirit. For most people, orgasm is a release. Too much release is abusive. It's not about releasing, but holding on to the present moment. It's important to compose and sustain one's own energy. It's the art of the physical carnality and sensuality coming together. This is where the true riches live. When we have abusive sexual relations, it builds toxins that need to be flushed out. The physical act and the height of climax is part of our creativity and community. The intense feeling, that being the push and pull is also the containment and sustainment. It's the way you perform the physicality that makes the release pure. *There's the sexual heart and then, there is the Kama Sutra.*

The Kama Sutra

The Kama Sutra has been widely published and followed as the popular sex book and has fallen into this category on a permanent basis. The book was written approximately 1600 years ago in India by the author, Vatsyayana. Within its many pages, there are details about the many kissing techniques, courting practices, modes of touching, sexual positions, asana and more. Originally written as a self help manual, the Kama Sutra, due to its explicit illustrations came across as Hindu pornography, but in fact, was offered as a treatise on the science of sexuality. The book went on to explain who to have affairs with, how to entertain johns in style, and how to acquire the right kind of "sugar daddy."

Vatsyayana's goal was to teach people to slow down and seize the moment, even to the point of encouraging them to re-decorate their homes so as to please the senses, (flowers, incense, beautiful art, soft fabrics, cushions and music.) It talked about inviting friends over while getting a little flirtation going on with the one you love then, after everyone leaves, the real lovemaking begins. He encouraged the use of oils, treats, drinking from each other's cup to help keep balance for balance (yin and yang). In this day and age, we practice Kama Sutra preparations.

There is a difference between Buddhist and Hindu Tantra. What makes them different is the form of deities, the meditations on psychic veins and airs, the fire rituals and so on. The philosophy and depth filled sources differ in the Buddhist and Hindu tantras. Buddhist tantra is superior because of three principles of the path, which include renunciation, the enlightened attitude, and the right philosophy.

To learn the heart requires discipline, courage, commitment, hard work, and intelligence. Love requires discipline so that one can unconditionally love. To have heart and tantra, it takes effort, commitment and soul. The idea is to choose a path that works best for you. The Vajrayana path is the most complex. It requires a well integrated sense of the self. Vajrayana is often viewed as the third, major vehicle, (Yana) of Buddhism and means "diamond vehicle." Tibetan Buddhism was found in Tibet, Bhutan, Northern India, Nepal, southwestern and northern China. Vajrayana Buddhism is a part of Tibetan Buddhism but Vajrayana specifically refers to tantra. Vajrayana claims to provide an accelerated path to enlightenment. This is achieved through the use of tantra techniques, which are practical aids to spiritual development, and esoteric transmission.

Vajrayana techniques identify enlightenment within the body, speech, and mind of a Buddha. To get there, one must begin with a strong, well integrated sense of the self. Tantra is a powerful path that can bring great joy. The key to Tantra is not to misuse or abuse its powers. It is to become free. To be authentic in Tantra; requires commitment, discipline, intelligence, courage, and a sense of wild, fool hardy and the unknown. Tantra is discipline and hard work. It molds the power of creation and ego into skillful means, cutting through delusion. To do real Tantra requires patience and time. The power of Tantra requires vulnerability. To be authentic, one must burn. Tantra is powered by one's own creative force. One must make room for the Tantric path. In other words, to stay on the Tantric path is a journey and if the divine is tampered with, bad karma results.

The divinity of life is sacred and must be valued. This often means looking at one's potential in manifesting their gifts to the universe and allowing their energy to set forth. The authentic self requires commitment, discipline, courage and a sense of wild liberation. These are the Tantric tools. To be Tantric, one must be the fool and yet be the initiator. Tantric sadhana deconstructs and constructs reality as play, until the essence of reality becomes obvious. The Tantric life is challenging in that one must let go, over and over again. Let go of what? One must let go of the force that takes you away from the soul. In this, the emptiness creates more potential. When we are empty, we can be wild and a whole new world of perception explodes from this pure potential which is also pure awareness.

The enlightened path we are on has the requirement that we are to teach empowerment—to make us live from the self, rather than without the whole. Empowerment and enlightenment begin with a shift. A shift from where you were born, how, into what energy space, into what planets and time, and what direction you were guided. Tantra is about controlling and directing one's sexual energies toward the greater goal. It is about creating a path for yourself, seeing where it is that you are being directed to go, being able to open to this path, seeing in others what you see in yourself and honoring this by allowing that sense of the self to be real.

"Undulation frees us from the bondage of the world while still living in it." – Anita

A song by Frank Natale, (a blind man from Australia), entitled, *Dance Connect Us All*, is powerful and moving in that it implies that all bodies are connected. So, in group sex, people look for this and understand the concept but, again, they lack emotional content. Dance brings us to a level of exhilaration and stimulates our emotions so that bodies can connect. It's the way a body celebrates.

"The sexual revolution disconnected us." – Anita

I believe that fantasies of a sexual nature are healthy to experiment with because they help us clear our minds of unnecessary energy that blocks the senses. *It's all about breaking up sexual tension.* Too much tension often takes the form of suppressed sexual energy. This tension needs to be relieved from the experience of the body. This is what the science of Kinepathics is about. Fantasies are merely thoughts that we allow to manifest in a physical way. The dance helps me express my thoughts and could only come from my sensual energy, which is my true spirit. Carnal expression has the same formula. We get a sexual thought, then a feeling, and eventually, act it out. The body's energy is the sensual energy. We need the inner feeling to act as a foundation. Without it, the physical act of loving can be almost abusive.

Fantasies are subconscious failures to measure up to what we think we need that springs from the conscious mind. Liberation allows this to play out, if at least in part, in our minds. At the time of the sexual revolution, sex was the metaphor for people wanting to connect, but instead, emotions were left hanging, thereby people grew further apart.

I believe that divorce, prostitution and even bisexuality have increased due to the lack of emotional nourishment from that era. In the Roman days, orgies were a natural way of life. I am not saying that that is the way. I just believe it's not something to look down upon. Communal living and polyamorous lifestyles are popular these days, and are growing. It can be very nourishing. People have claimed a winning chance in the land of opportunity and this is why sexual freedom became so popular. The power of the pelvis is where it all began—the seed of the womb. It's the "real" self. People want to prostitute themselves with people in power because it's a way of tying into the sense of the self. Such liberation is a way of honoring the God within.

"I am liberated because 'I CAN BE '." – Anita

Philosophies & Lessons from Chapter 5

Philosophies

Rigidity is a disease where we neglect the expression that creates those walls. Rigid people hold themselves stiff with pride. They have a challenge surrendering to emotion. They hold back, thus holding their physical selves back. They limit their expression. Rigidity keeps the fear of being suppressed alive, neglecting resiliency. Other body types are oral, rigid, psychopathic, schizoid, histrionic, masochistic and hysterical, to name a few. The deeper the heart opens for rigid types, the more they let down their defenses.

It's when two people meet that their emotions are at such a frenzied level that they tend to go over the edge. It's about that space between two people, the space of freedom—connection. It's about being there with all that energy crackling like lightning before a storm; before falling over the edge—that bond that keeps you true to yourself. It's a boundary of energy that we control, bringing it out when we want, drawing it back in when we need it. To allow yourself to be wild is to allow your reality to expand even further before slipping over the edge. It's perfectly okay when you come back.

Resistance is healthy because it is the masculine that formulates grounding. Resistance provides a foundation of strength. However, resistance must be accompanied with fluidity—the push and pull of life. When we push, we flow and know when to let go of the resistance. The rhythm of emotions is the cure. Going beyond the edge of resistance, is to let go, feeling it all the way.

When we are ourselves, the circumstances of the world oppress us, because we freely liberate our emotions. The fact that we do, should liberate others. In some instances, it draws out the fear and jealousy. I want to encourage those of you out there to "be who you are" and live life to its fullest.

When you are the "real you," then you experience life. How beautiful is the dirt on the ground and the beauty in all of us.

Lessons Learned

Rape taught me about personalities. I learned that rape happens among the rich and famous and we never hear about it.

I learned that when violence happens, it's because the emotions shifted to a point of non-reality. Lots of people stay angry at themselves for being vulnerable but I learned to accept this emotion as a part of myself.

I learned to shift back to my center and into the person and world I wanted at any given moment. I learned so much about life working in Jazz radio. It was a part of my therapy and a big part of my life.

CHAPTER 6

୧୨ଡ଼

Understanding the Kinepathics Process
Introduction

"Learning is what I do, dreams are what I breathe." – Anita

Man's purpose on this great planet of ours is to recreate and refine his spirit. Having a spiritual life simply means learning how to die and how to let go of what you don't want or need. It's learning how to be in the spirit—in the moment.

Wisdom unfolds on many levels and often does, happening within the reality of suffering, as it did for me. I believe people are afraid to face the fact that life comes and goes; of their own mortality. It is why we face so much suffering. It's okay to live and die when we know we continue to live in someone else. Your spirit is alive in everyone. The goal is to be alive through the God in all of us. God is the presence of good and the action of love. To feel the presence in yourself, to worship your higher power and praise others is considered of great value. It is that value that has yet to be realized.

We need to learn to teach people who they are by helping them awaken their minds. Tell them what you think. Boldly teach them who they are and help them come face to face with this truth. When you can accomplish this, your shame and sorrows will be relieved. This is done in many ways and forms. Rap singer, Eminem did it through his music. You can't know how great it feels to you express your thoughts to another person about who they are. However, it must be done with constructive criticism and love, not hate, venting or projecting negatively. Keep in mind that we are the projectors of our own movies, whether negative or positive. People have a tendency to go on projecting their negative emotions and their spiritual insufficiencies onto others as a way of gaining power and remaining in denial.

Now, you know how to see things for what they are. There is a part of love that people don't understand. It is, simply, that intimacy heals. When you have a relationship with your feelings and are sharing this intimacy with another, it teaches people about their truth. When you are awakened, you know who you are; or are at least letting go of denial and shame. The focus needs to be more on helping each other. That is the most important job of being a human—and our responsibility.

Martin Luther King was a great promoter of this type of thinking. He wanted to end segregation and racial discrimination by raising public consciousness from a political point of view. The biggest problem that plagues the world, generation by generation, is our inability to accept and balance ethnicity and religion. This tragic imbalance causes us to suppress each other by allowing it to continue. If King were around today, he could, quite possibly, be one of the great spiritual leaders of the new age movement—perhaps, even president of the United States. I am proud to have experienced on my 52nd birthday, November 4, 2008 the election of Obama. That is one birthday I won't forget.

If the way he approached issues then, politically, was done today, his ideas would have gone over much better. We have come a long way in thinking in the consciousness of the new age, since then. King was barely scratching the surface in his day. All it takes is a strong leader. There is a strong leader in every one of us. We just need to take charge.

After he visited India, King deepened his understanding of non-violent resistance to America's struggle for civil rights. He became aware of his karma and enlightenment, thus clearing the way for a new way of thinking. This is what we all need to do. We need to cleanse our karma from the damage of the past, so that it keeps moving forward, merging as one. We also have to rid ourselves of the feeling of fear that permeates our lives, so that the pure and natural love within us can shine through. Then you will understand that we are all part of a collective consciousness.

The song, *Cleaning Out Your Closet*, sung by Eminem, means 'surrendering to what is now and what possibilities are yet to come.' King got a piece of the Hindu way of thinking when he began to honor the divine in all of creation. Hinduism is the religious practice in India.

The Hindu way of life is a liberal one that freely gives space and freedom to every individual. King needed to make White America understand that, when the blacks suffered, we all suffered. What is sad to know, is that people vote for presidents and politicians according to their race or gender, rather than their ability to make healthy, positive changes. Frequently, I hear people ask;

"Are we ready for a female or black president?"

When we are free from this prejudicial type of thinking, that question won't exist. The world is entering a new movement—one of love, honoring the mother earth, as well as the nature of the male and female in all of us. King was assassinated for his liberal way of thinking and his openness to humanity.

Sexuality is also repressed in our culture. Expression and love are a beautiful part of the sexual energetic movement. When we restrict people, we are creating more violence, which surfaces in the world.

Dr. Wilhelm Reich, a respected analyst that worked with the character structure of people, was on a movement to change people one by one, however, not from a political view. He worked with people like, Fritz Perls, Freud and others. Reich was viewed by the psychoanalytic establishment as having gone astray in his wild, liberal way of thinking and was later condemned by the courts for his progressive work. He believed that a court was not the proper place, in which to decide matters of science, and was sent to jail, where he eventually died.

The point I'm making is that we have come a long way, but politics still rule every little aspect of life. The political world needs to be able to accept change as it stands on the precipice, ready to enter into the feminine energy of life. It is this change that the world desperately needs. When this change occurs there will be a decrease in greed, which would help people to heal. *We are all suffering from the politics and segregation of one kind or another.* When there is a subtle gentle change in politics, people, in general, will be more loving. Unfortunately, the hearts of politicians still remain closed. It is when hearts are open that anything is possible.

This change is all about how much you value life and the importance of honoring yourself. It is the God within us that needs to be honored. Don't wait for someone else to praise you. Begin by praising yourself in every moment. Be mindful, yet open. Sometimes, the heart can get confused, but deep down inside us, we know the truth. We can only face that reality when we "empty our cup" so-to-speak. By emptying the cup, you are clearing out the tubes, relearning. When we understand the difference, we know our power. This is the strength inside us.

Stop looking to presidents and politicians to make the world a better place. It's up to you to assist and teach them on their journey to becoming part of the collective help. Let go of your excuses and enter the moment. This is "presence." Yet, I still hear people say;

"Well, let's see what this mayor is going to do for our city."

Instead of waiting, take the time to acknowledge this person. Assist them by doing what you can to set the city on a forward movement of change. People suffer because they fight for respect of themselves. Once you start loving yourself, that war will end. Though hard to believe, we truly are fighting with ourselves, not others. We tend to project outward that way when the fight has always been within.

Choose love not fear. To love, we need to be free, have an open heart. We need to surrender to our foundation. Open your heart and be one with the universe. Only then will you be free from suffering. The Divine enters us in a way we all understand; the way in which we connect.

Reichian therapy was developed by Wilhelm Reich, M.D. His therapy is a method of character transformation that recognizes the essential identity of the mind and body. It is known as "Orgone" therapy, which is a method to reduce the walls we build in our body, essentially suppressing feelings that once existed, but couldn't find a way to be expressed. Armoring, or "putting up walls," blocks "free expression." This work progresses by gradually reducing the "armor" and charging up the body to discharge, thus releasing anger. It honors the very pulse of life. It is a ripple that can go on forever. Reichian therapy is an emotional release set of exercises, otherwise known as, somatic psychology. Somatic refers to the experience within emotion. Releasing the anger promotes natural vitality, sexuality and an overall joy of life through Orgone breathing and movement. We were taught to hold back our basic needs and feelings, which we've learned are inappropriate. It takes a lot of energy to hold back what comes naturally, thus developing chronic muscular tension.

I discovered Reich's work when I was about 12 years old. It was when my mother asked me to do this breathing method with her. She had studied the dramatic arts, so she had some insight into the emotional world. She also understood the body environment. She would lie down on her back and breathe loud and deep, then kick and punch and throw a temper tantrum. Then she'd ask me to look her in the eyes, making a deep connection with her.

Next, I studied Dr. Alexander Lowens's Bioenergetics work. As a witness to my mother's somatic emotional processing experience, I learned how the body moved from within—how it undulated.

It wasn't until I was 20 that I learned about tantra yoga. Innately, I knew it was about the divine and love. However, my first teacher showed me tantra in a negative way. Not too much later, I met a Swami, whom I asked to explain to me, all about tantra and the divine. He proceeded to tell me one thing, but do another. He also tried to have me believe that tantra was just about sex, but I knew better. I was aware, by now, that tantra promoted love and the spirit and that sex was the ultimate power only after one achieved this. Undulation is what I wanted more of. So, I learned that somatic movement exercises, was the journey I needed to pursue, in order to understand more about the innate body. This led me to kinesiology movement studies.

"At the dawn of civilization, dance and movement were an expression of healing, ritual, culture, and life celebration. It's the primal nature where the body was born and lives within its natural movement. Modern society has forced the human character to live in unnatural ways, causing a split between body, mind and spirit. In the forefront of nature; life presents many possibilities exploring frontiers, experiencing depth, and allowing the human senses to be realized."

Kinesiology is a popular scientific study of anatomy, physiology and the mechanics of body movement. It was this part of the puzzle that had me intrigued. I began to study the connective tissue. I desired to know how and why the body moved the ways that it did. Working as an X-ray technologist helped me understand the anatomy of our physical forms and the psychology of the soul. I realized that the connective tissue sent messages to the brain, allowing us to make personality changes. The connective tissue became stimulated through the movement, "undulations" that I had taught myself while in CHH. However, it was the emotional center that captivated me more than anything, and between the two, emotional and physical; I realized there was a connection. The connective tissue needed to be stimulated by way of the emotions and body movement. I realized that, to be free from conditioned responses, I needed to embrace them with awareness. I taught myself to be "present" and experience my senses. I worked with the wave motion of undulation which increased the electrical charge in my connective tissue.

I first discovered the kinesthetic movement of the body during my x-ray technology training. The movement, inner organs and connective tissue, which is made up of the amazing fascia, is what creates pathways in the body.

Fascia is the soft tissue component of the extensive tissue system that permeates the entire human body. It is an uninterrupted, three-dimensional web of tissue extending from head to toe, front to back and interior to exterior. This tissue maintains structural integrity; providing support and protection as well as acting as a shock absorber. Fascia functions as the body's first line of defense against pathogenic agents and infections. After an injury has occurred, it is the fascia that creates an environment for tissue repair.

I became a great observer of life and began my journey to seek out answers; what's, where's, why's, and who's. Seekers are the people who believed themselves worthless, who were suppressed of their powers and maintaining that belief, so that another could be in falsity. We are born innocent, and present. The normal, wholesome, healthy mind is already in existence within the enlightened mind. When we shift, we make a difference. The universe is constantly shifting and we don't even know it. Now, we are being forced to look at the reality, the moment.

There is no beginning or end. It's the here and now that matters. People often ask;

"How does one become more aware?"

It begins with a journey and a purpose. First, you become a seeker of life—in search of your destiny—placing your life on a pedestal while seeking the divine of life, when, suddenly, a shift happens. Developing a connection with one another, while being more aware of the environment and the planet, which raises our levels of consciousness to the truth, and which is the innate power. Trusting ourselves and others is a big part of it. I know that trusting others out there in the world can be risky, but when we are whole, we know exactly how much we can trust and how much of ourselves we can extend. It's important that we do it with healthy boundaries. When we apply meaning to our experiences, we make conscious choices. Having choices is empowering. *When we let go of what we perceive as needs, happiness and self worth, we find lasting power.*

Love is a divine nature of existence. Love is the wealth. Becoming rich in our heart is what our true desires are, and yet we bury them behind external barriers. We assault our own emotions, refusing to acknowledge them. We take the time to prepare for the big holidays such as Thanksgiving and Christmas. We make all these preparations for just one day. What we don't recognize, is that life is but one day—one big day of celebrations from the highest to the low. Take enough time out and extend your life by "smelling the roses." When we are in "process," we extend the moments of our existence. Opening your heart to your own feelings, instead of someone else's feelings, is the first step. This helps to end our isolation from our own feelings, from those of others and the higher power. Boundaries are important, but you will pay a hefty price when they are up all the time. Be careful not to build walls around the heart, because when the heart is not stimulated, we shut down our ability to feel pleasure. *Hate comes from people suppressing one another.*

We need to heal from the segregation that we've been exposed to—to make a move from segregation to integration. Society, today, lacks the base for finding solutions in necessary reality. People suppress each other because they harbor resentment. They resent some of what they see in themselves, so they suppress others. To break free, we must be aware. When we experience total freedom, there is only awareness. The more we work on becoming more conscious, the easier life gets and all the misery fades away. All I ever wanted was love. So, I fell in love with my heart, this is where the ultimate understanding begins. You, too, can make love to you. Love yourself.

> **"I'm in love with the truth, that's what's so funny about me.
> In 'presence,' we are all equal." – Anita**

Kinepathics was created from all the things I learned from the age of nine, at CHH when all I could move of my body was from my pelvis to my head in a wave like motion—the undulations of my body and my emotions, thus healing myself.

Kinepathics (ki ná path iks) is an occidental philosophy that originates from the Greek words, "kinesis" meaning a movement or activity of a cell or an organism in response to a stimulus; and "pathos" meaning emotions and the way of expression and disease. Kinepathics means to move the disease out of the body through the emotional connection of the senses.

Kinepathics promotes self-liberation, love and an understanding of who you are.

I realized that the emotions and thoughts were connected to the tissues of the body and that, within the muscle, was our armor—the unexpressed voice. Kinepathics is part of my "thoughted motion," and is a concept of my innateness. When we think negative thoughts, we grow weak; when we feed ourselves negative words, we lose inner strength. When we think positive thoughts, we become stronger, physically, innately, and finally, emotionally.

Kinepathics integrates segregation by bringing together the emotional, physical, mental, sensual, and spiritual value of the human condition. This method works from the senses, enabling individuals to bond with the self and transform from the subconscious mind, thereby connecting to the conscious mind. To perform Kinepathics, is to strive for the truth; to continually become a better person—to seek out your desires and contribute your share to life.

These exercises are a form of discipline to help you redefine your body—to look at your soul and get to know who you are, "the real you." It is a study of the self—a teaching of one's inner beliefs. Kinepathics develops our authenticity, sharpens the senses and creates an awareness of a higher power that can only be sought "in the experience." Kinepathics was born out of my own life experiences, from desire, truth, and passion. The Kinepathics Method of Life Solutions is an approach designed to help develop your inner world and create a foundation for change, direction and balance.

The Kinepathics Approach

I.   The Relationship to Your Feelings

II.   Self Discipline/Motivation

III.   Breath Alive

IV.   Body, Mind, Sexual Awareness

V.   Communication

VI.   Liberation – WildDance™

NOTE: Keep in mind that this approach to kinepathics is a guideline. This is a compilation of many different practices. Naturally, these are best done in my group workshops and private sessions. However, I am aware that not everyone is able to do this. I encourage you to practice alone or with a partner. You can practice all or some of these exercises and you can mix them around. A good way to practice is, to either take one step at a time and focus on that for a month, or take one exercise from each step and work on that. To become who you are, it is best to practice what feels right for you. These exercises require time to develop properly. Repetition and practice will help you delve deeper within yourself. I will have a DVD later on this.

CHAPTER 7

ℜ

Kinepathics Approach
The Real Self

The Relationship to Your Feelings

To begin in life, we must first love and understand ourselves, know thyself, be thyself, have a strong relationship with the self, as if you're the only person that exists in the world. Have you ever examined your relationship to your own feelings? Along the way, you may have lost love of the self due to negative experiences and environments. It is important to love the body strongly before you love anything else. Cultivate your relationship to yourself first. To be successful, you must re-learn how to open your heart and truly love again. In order to enjoy good family and healthy relationships, it is essential to take on a spiritual practice every day, even if it is sitting quietly for a few moments. Being the "real self" requires focus and commitment. The first step is to love yourself no matter what you've been through or what you're going through right now.

- NOTES -

Forgiveness

Forgive the self, then others, and you will begin to see the real self. When you forgive yourself and others, you truly begin to live. As we forgive, we take the action to do so from our inner power. Forgive others for yourself, not for them. Forgiveness is an art of the heart. I know that sometimes that we have a lot of resentment so that forgiving does not come easily, but if you hold onto the pain, you stay on the edge of anger and end up living with resentment and resistance. When we forgive we develop the ability to interact with resistance. Resentment is a part of the negative emotion in anger and is felt as a result of real or imagined wrong done to us at one time or another. When we feel resentment, a major part of the self closes. Resentment breeds bitterness, which leads to hate, which affects our ability to express love. Forgiveness is the first step to healing. Forgive your mother, your father, past lovers, and finally, yourself. Forgive them their limited abilities to know better. In order to rid ourselves of resentment, we need to forgive the person that made us feel this way.

Love Thyself

You need to prepare so that you will feel the love for yourself or you won't feel it for anyone. The strongest relationship there is, is the relationship to the self—the relationship with your feelings. People claim they love themselves, or ask how they know that they love themselves? It takes a lot of willpower to love the self more and more each day. It is the first and most important relationship that one must cultivate before moving onto loving another. Accept yourself and the life you were given.

As a powerful force of nature, love should be cherished and respected within all of us.

The way you begin is by searching for the truth within yourself. Love is a discovery that goes beyond ordinary thoughts. Loving yourself is an integral part of surrendering yourself and your ego to a greater reality. The love of the self is there, but you must dig for it if you want to be "real." As a result of loving the self, you will be able to feel closer to your feminine and masculine energies. That comes when we understand our underlying animal. Animals are accepting of their nature and their sexuality, which makes them as one with the universe. We are always in constant love with the self with the yin/yang, complimenting each other. To love the self, we must free ourselves from the traumas of our past. We must let go of the baggage. Begin by clearing out your home of the junk.

Honor Thy Body

Your body is like a holy temple. You must respect it. The body temple contains your energy. If we don't honor, praise and love the body then who will? People will walk all over you if you allow them. Loving the body is the truth that connects us to the universe. When we are connected this way, the truth just exists making further searching unnecessary. The body is the place you come home to everyday. It's your primary residence. It's your ray of light, your temple, your tabernacle. If you don't accept your body then your actions are not "real." Part of accepting the body self, is reflection. The body has its own innate intelligence—the power of your being—your brain. The body and mind have been connecting for a long time in the new age. Now is the time to bring your spirit back to life because it is this, which revolves around the sexual self. Allow your powers to flow accordingly and praise your own sense of inner beauty. Allow your body to breathe, live and enter its divine nature of truth. Take a chance and step out on the path and enlighten your senses with your own feelings. Your body is the divine nature of God. Be careful of the words you feed yourself, they are absorbed into the body space. When we learn to function from the source, with love, then we begin the steps to becoming sacred. Herein, is found the body voice.

Developing Giving & Receiving

Giving and receiving require joint cooperation for any kind of relationship to happen. When we do one, then the other happens. It is about balancing your happiness and your energy. When we are aware, we can understand this concept. The goal is to understand how to direct your given energy. Once you are familiar with your energy, you can learn how to direct it—the push/pull effect.

When your body is open and free, then you are able to accept the gifts. Some people have difficulty receiving, because they don't feel worthy. Being receptive teaches our soul about the essence of life. Receive with your heart and give with love. To receive is to open yourself to the universe and receive what it provides for you. When you receive, you increase your relationship to the self even more, because you trust your soul. Receiving involves listening to the silence. To give from the heart, not the ego is the ultimate in giving—the act of giving and not expecting anything in return. When you are able to give in that way then, you are ready to receive. So, you want to give but you don't know how. Take a look at yourself in the mirror and see how beautiful you are, then acknowledge what it is you have that others want and bring that out from your heart. Know your gifts, receive them for yourself, and then share them with others.Be careful of giving too deeply, or you'll experience a lack of self preservation and innateness. When we give too deeply, our energy is scattered and needs to be re-directed. Adjustments need to be created.

Harnessing Aloneness

When you are alone, the relationship to the self grows stronger. It's okay to be alone and not feel empty, but rather content—enjoying your own company. Honor these moments. The spirit will become more "present." Being in the alone is experiencing the distance between life and death. Aloneness is a state of being in life. When we experience being in the alone, then you have reached the most successful form of integration you can have with yourself. Loneliness is a tool we use toward understanding the self more intimately—to surrender fear and hostility.

It is the behavior of one who knows the self and sees the pardons objectifying with nature's eyes in order to bring about an injustice that spreads with the ferocity of the loss of insanity.

Loneliness is wisdom, because you recognize the identity of the self with feeling. Loneliness is a connection to the outside if we let go. It's an opening to your gift that attracts the rebels residing stationary within. Being in the alone is freedom. Once you adapt to the silence of your loneliness, you will have conditioned the body to maintain a level of calmness. Then, when you are faced with "the noise," your body will not panic. The sense of true flow in the body will block the noise. To "be in the alone" is the true wisdom of individual freedom.

When I focus, it is on everything that I do, not just the main goal. Focus is everything. This aloneness is power. As the loner liberates independence, he welcomes love.

- PRACTICE -

1) FORGIVE: No partner needed. Make a list of the people, going back to your childhood that you want to forgive. Write a letter and, if possible, set up a visit. Remember, you're doing this for you. Make a list of all the things that you want to forgive in yourself. Then, forgive yourself for holding back and not doing the things that you could have done. Write down all the things you want to forgive in anyone else including the universe.

2) ROLE PLAY: Partner necessary. One person sits on a chair while the other kneels down. Let this person, who is sitting, represent a past lover, or parent or anyone you want to forgive. Personalize the situation by calling out their name, and imagine that this is that person who caused you pain. Forgive them in your own words for the pain they have caused you. If you don't have a person to work with, place a teddy bear or material object on a chair and let that represent this person. Forgive the imaginary person with all your heart and then take some quiet moments to reflect.

3) MEDITATION: No partner needed. Sit everyday in a cross-legged, comfortable position for 20 minutes in meditation. Alternate between the morning and evening to do this. Add the mantra: "I am one with the self," "I love myself." Later you will find your own mantra. Have eyes closed and do not lie down. Later on you can find meditation in an activity such as cooking.

4) IN THE MOMENT: No partner needed. Sit with one hand on the heart area and the other on the lower belly. For 10 minutes, 3 times a week, use the words: "I am love, love is all that I am, I am the love of my life, love creates me, God, create in me a clean heart." Resonate with the heartfelt connection. Now, add breathing to that feeling; Breathe in through your nose and out through your mouth. Later add your own mantra wording.

5) LET GO: No partner needed. Let go of two television programs this month. Let go of a distraction in your life. Could be a phone friend that complains too much. Focus on what it is that you really want in your life—what you want to enter your being. Watch a distraction disappear from your psyche. Focus on what you love about yourself.

6) HYDROTHERAPY: No partner needed. Take a very cold shower followed by a hot shower once a week then, wrap yourself in a blanket and sit in a dark, quiet room. If you are unable to do this once a week, at least do it once a month. You may find a gym that has a cold plunge and Jacuzzi. This would work.

7) MIRROR BREATHING: No partner needed. Stand in front of the mirror. We are going to do "Orgone" breathing techniques. Standing tall with your hands in the air over your head, face the mirror and breathe in through the mouth and exhale through the mouth with hands falling down to the side on the exhale. Keep the mouth vertically wide open, and with eyebrows going up and down, begin to take 10 deep breaths in and out. Then, when you feel you can do no more, bend your body with your head folded over toward the knees and eventually onto the floor onto your knees in a child's pose . This would be face down with knees folded in toward the chest and arms to the side and forehead on the mat. If a partner is near have them rub your back muscles around the neck and spine.

8) SELF WORSHIP: No partner needed. Fill the tub with Epsom salts and some soothing bubble bath. Set the environment with a candle and soft music. Prepare to take the time to be alone and worship the self. Afterward, wrap yourself in a blanket and sit quietly. You may want to listen to soft soothing music or listen to your quiet thoughts.

9) INTENTION VOICE: No partner needed. For every person you look at today, repeat to yourself the mantra: "I love that person" and "I love that person for who they are." This will help block the judgmental thoughts that, otherwise, arise.

10) MIRROR TALK: No partner needed. While looking in your eyes in the mirror, recite:

> *"I deserve to love and be loved."*
>
> *"I deserve to receive the gifts of the universe."*
>
> *"I deserve to have a wonderful mate."*
>
> *" Everyone loves me"*

11) GIVING: No partner needed. Practice giving and receiving in 5 different situations this week. Give a smile, give love, and give a kind word; lend a hand, give a coin, a hug and give a thought.

12) TOUCH: Partner necessary. Sit across from a partner and delicately provide touch to their arms. Express how you like to be touched from an emotional and physical view. You need to close your eyes and receive. Then reverse. Do for 5 minutes each.

13) MIRROR WITNESS: No partner needed. Stand in front of a mirror and look at who you are. Take time to really see yourself clearly. Check in with your feelings. Pick five things about yourself that you accept presently and five things that you accepted about yourself when you were a child. Personalize the statements with your own name when looking in the mirror. For example, "I ____ accept being alone. I___ accept that I wasn't really accepted as a child." And then state things about yourself that you love. Take five things from the present and the past. For example: "I___ love my body and the way I keep it in shape today, I___ loved when I was in eleventh grade and I got a standing ovation for a play." How I can help make myself better is_____

14) SELF ESTEEM: No partner needed. Stand in front of mirror in the nude or clothed and do a bragging exercise, saying ten things you like about your body. This will help you feel good about yourself and boost your body image. It is important to be proud of you, and it breaks shame.

15) BREATH OF FIRE: No partner needed. Sitting in a cross-legged position while flexing and extending the spine, breathe in and out of the nose forcefully with lips sealed. Do this for 10 minutes.

16) THE FACE MASK: No partner needed. To unleash false feelings and soften the facial muscles. First, begin to rotate the neck in any way that feels comfortable. Let the neck free fall with eyes closed. Then, place the fingers on the head and assist the movement of the head and neck. Continue for as long as needed.

17) BREATHE OUT THE ANGER: No partner needed. Sit in a chair and close your eyes. We will do orgone energy breath. Breathe in and out of the mouth deeply—long, deep breaths and track your energy. Begin by acknowledging what you're feeling from your ankles up to your knees, from your knees to your pelvis, from your belly button to your heart, to your head and then go down the back of the body. Track the energy from the neck down the back to the hips, from the hips down the hamstrings and down the calves and the back of the feet. Then open your eyes and just relax.

18) ALONE TIME: No partner needed. Take 30 minutes a week to be alone and experience your feelings without interruptions. This can increase your self awareness of being in the present moment. This is a good time to focus on your relations with other people, your senses and listening to your heart. Make a conscious connection with the heartbeat.

CHAPTER 8

❧

Kinepathics Approach
The Creative Self

Self Discipline / Self Motivation

Self discipline takes practice and time. This doesn't mean reprimanding yourself or a child, it simple means having and containing the willpower that is in you. It is a form of motivation that guides us toward containment and responsibility. It is the internal focus that makes you the leader of your life. Punishing a child is not disciplining them, Discipline comes from a deeper internal place of truth. When you love someone, there is discipline. This structuring of self control begins in your everyday life, in the way you think, walk and manage your life. Discipline is learning how to be an optimist and how to develop hope for all humanity. It is responsibility.

Former football coach, Vince Lombardi, once said that *"The difference between a successful person and others is not a lack of strength, not a lack of knowledge, but rather a lack of will."*

- NOTES -

Developing Willpower

Willpower is the essential energy of our deepest being. To exercise willpower is to set a course of action and follow it through. This energy is the inner strength that defines our passion and boost for life. It is a concentration of force guided by positive energy. When you use willpower, you gather your energy and exert it with confidence. The more experience you gain, the more willpower you gain. Exerting your will means pulling your energy in, and knowing when to let it out again.

Willpower goes hand in hand with discipline. It is the ability to control unnecessary, harmful impulses and overcome procrastination. Procrastination manifests as confusion, a type of paralysis which indicates a lack of self love. It is our inner power that overcomes the desire to indulge in unnecessary and useless habits. The inner strength that is developed to overcome emotional and mental resistance is fueled by willpower. Once we develop the inner self, our intuitive senses are sharpened, thus the will to live becomes stronger. This intuition is a spiritual companion to life. Self discipline helps us withdraw from our hardships and difficulties and is used in conjunction with willpower to keep us from acting out rashly, rather to see the big picture and, therefore, solve those problems in a positive way.

Both forces grant the ability to reject immediate satisfaction in lieu of waiting for something better. They are a balance of the subconscious and conscious mind. Sometimes we think about one thing, do something else, which makes us feel another way. It is all too easy to end up later regretting something we said or did. When willpower and discipline have reached maturity, we become conscious of our inner subconscious impulses. So, we train the mind to accept and reject what is necessary under both circumstances. The goal is to align our thoughts, feelings, and actions and have control over them. First, we have self discipline then, willpower. It's a learning experience to use the two together. Cutting out some of the indulgences is a way of exercising discipline. Willpower gets stronger when we learn to hold back the unimportant and unhealthy thoughts, feelings, actions and reactions. The two forces, when in balance with our being, serve to strengthen us. Denial has to be the most challenging part of developing willpower. We measure our actions and reactions then, train them as we would our muscles. Willpower gives us control and management when we truly desire something that isn't necessary for us. When willpower and discipline cleanse the body, it allows love to surface.

Permit love to be the strength that gives you the will to go forward. Reflect on the areas in your life that need willpower so you will know where your strengths and weaknesses lie. It's about surrendering to your desire and going beyond. The idea is to have complete control of your thoughts and direct your energy your own way. In order to strengthen your willpower, practice the eight fold path of yoga to become free, by using discipline to let go of unhealthy attachments.

Healing Your Losses (Baggage)

Many of us tend to hold on to the negative experiences in our lives for years without knowing what we are holding onto or why. When we reflect through meditation, we come to understand why, and know what we are holding onto so that it becomes easier to let go of. Holding patterns are stored within the nervous system. When we keep our past traumas within, we are sometimes driven by fear and hate. If we train ourselves a little each day to let go of transference, we step a little closer toward who we are. We step up to the plate, so-to-speak. Baggage, or all the negative experiences we keep within us, is the biggest obstacle preventing us from truly being who we are. If traumatic events are not processed emotionally when they occur, they will eventually pile up; creating musculature armor that causes us to behave defensively. When we are defensive, it's like carrying baggage that fills us so that we are only half a person. People that live with and carry all that negativity around, literally, live cluttered lives.

Examine your home, you might notice how much clutter you live with. When you go out, are you the type to bring home lots of unnecessary bags and paraphernalia? It can take many years before someone realizes that their lives hide trauma they never realized had happened, as well as transference which can be passed on from when they were in the womb, and later from their parents. This kind of baggage keeps a person emotionally unable to cope, leading to depression—imprisoned. Half the people of the world carry some sort of baggage. When we breathe into the place where we're mired, it is there we bring conscious awareness and allow life to be present also.

Some of us are filled with so much pain that it has become a natural way of life. When we release baggage from the muscled character, your personality will begin to change and you will unfold like the layers of a flower, recreating a new person—a new you. Your goal becomes understanding your body and how your energy progresses in increments.

How much energy we have and how we use it determines the way we react to the stimulants in our lives. When the energy seems unavailable, we react from either the false ego, from fears, or from uncontrolled impulses. When we let go of the baggage, we free more energy and space.

Getting Beyond Your Boundaries

How do you relate to boundaries when you meet the earth? Do you dive in? Some of us create pain as a boundary. Others have no boundaries.

One of the most important things one can do in life is to respect another's boundaries. This is the moment. Why is it that we have so many boundaries? There are positive and negative boundaries which we are to identify in order to decide whether they are right for us. The more boundaries we have, the more rigid we become, trapping ourselves and squeezing off our freedom. Unhealthy boundaries are nothing but defenses that allow anxiety to multiply, breeding stress within.

Why do people have defenses? It's because they've been hurt and feel the need to protect themselves. Perhaps, they've never been loved and their defenses become a barrier of protection around the opening of their heart. It's time to put it behind you and move on.

It's healthy to set up some boundaries. So, we need to understand what a boundary is as well as what it isn't. First of all, I don't even use the word b___ in my vocabulary. Why? It's because the mind has risen to its superconscious level. You can become boundless. For example, if someone lies to you when you're in a committed relationship, would you consider this as crossing a boundary? Expressing it in terms of someone being dishonest is easier on the ears than to the musculature of crossing my boundaries. When we continually create boundaries within our frame, we are continually adding armor to the muscles—digging a deeper hole for the self. Letting go is about opening and receiving. Boundaries are, by far, the most important part of any relationship.

Let's look at healthy boundaries versus defensive boundaries. Defenses that are built from protecting the self lead to musculature armor. This armor takes away a person's ability to feel expression, creating resistance and anger to surface more often than not. People with defensive, false boundaries tend to understand their intuition but don't know how to let it live. Resistance grounds us so we need it to a point, because it helps one define and inhabit space. It's important to have resistance with fluid more so than resistance with armor. The goal is to break down the armor so we can rebuild and re-pattern the nervous system.

In loving relationships, boundaries are necessary so that we don't cling to our partners, but love them enough to give them space. If you give too much energy away, you lose identity; if you don't give enough, you lose reality. The goal is to learn, through Kinepathics, how to direct and move energy in a focused way, knowing when to stop, where to go, and for what length of time. Women tend to say they have no boundaries when it comes to sleeping with a new love interest. Boundaries are not our thoughts; however, they come from the strength in our soul. You need to know what you want in order to be secure and feel safe with your decisions. Once you know yourself better, boundaries become natural receptors that activate when necessary. These natural fences work with the ego by building a solid foundation within the soul. The more complete you become, the fewer boundaries you will need. It's about the law of attraction—attracting through the spirit.

Boundaries begin with communication skills. How effectively you communicate and how you deal with confrontation and assertiveness—how you interact with resistance. Resistance is a healthy tool for building necessary boundaries. Having too much resistance is in opposition to our natural electrical currents that send messages to the brain.

Valuing Relationships

Do you place value on your relationships? People come and go, so values in life always change. At one time, people cherished each other, loving each other for no other reason than to love. We need to get back the concept of unconditional love. However, love is harder to give these days. People take relationships of all kinds for granted. They see no more value in them as they attach importance to the materialistic things in life. Relationships are meant to be so we can provide support to one another, respect each other's contributions and cherish the sacred space in romantic love that two people hold together. The first thing about appreciating a relationship, is acknowledging it. You are responsible for the happiness and fulfillment it brings to you. This means letting go of the victim mentality so you can be strong in honoring, accepting, and becoming part of the relationship.

Understanding that there are risks and vulnerability is a part of growth. When we can be, "in the moment" of our true emotions so that we are able to show our vulnerabilities, we can admit that we are moving beyond our boundaries. It is then that you realize the force of growth. When we accept each other, we know the value of ourselves. This is because we see ourselves in the people we care about. Respect of the self allows us to value love even more. One way to signify your relationships, is to always look at the good—the positive. In your relationship with your parents, a lot of negative things were said and done over the years, but if you could reflect and remember the positive traits, you will discover that you thrived from them, instilling merit in you. Another way to value your relationships is, to come together in the healing of one another, listening, caressing, supporting, moving toward one another, taking the time to be present, to show compassion, and assist each other in overcoming your pain.

Always remember that with any relationship, there was friendship first, so you should always be friends. When we support one another, we aid in building one's self esteem, which is all a part of the nurturing process of life. Be aware of displaced angers that you may direct toward your partner. Instead, base your relationship upon integrity and not lies and deception. Learn how to communicate so you can say what you need to say. Support one another with healthy communication. Allow some time for yourself during the relationship. When we create space with intention, the attention will be there.

"Willpower is nothing but willingness to do." – BKS Iyengar

- PRACTICE -
The Eight Fold Path of Yoga
YAMA AND NIYAMAS DISCIPLINE

Yamas *(Restraints)*

In order to learn about the self and follow the tantric yoga path, one must first remove their negative behaviors, thoughts and actions. When we change our approach to life, we realize a beginning point for stress reduction.

- THE FIVE YAMAS -

1. Ahimsa *(Nonviolence)*

Letting go of negative self talk, judging the self and others and lack of self love is not healthy. An example of violence is, when a person takes advantage of another's good nature and feelings as some people do when having sex. We are to love another as we want to be loved, with truth and honesty. PRACTICE: Quit judging your partner and allow what's there to be present. Accept yourself. Replace one negative thought with a positive one toward yourself and your partner. Stop complaining.

2. Satya *(Truth)*

Silence is the non-violent means of expressing truth. Speaking clearly and honestly, even if it causes pain is truth. When you speak the truth, you are telling it like it is and being forthright. It is our birthright to transmit the message just as it is to fully receive it.

PRACTICE: Tell your partner something true about yourself that you may have lied about before. Come clean. Do this with your friends. Let them know who you really are.

3. Asteya *(Abstention From Stealing)*

One steals from the mother earth by not appreciating the goods that support life. Taking another's power for your own ego is stealing; not supporting another's good accomplishments is also stealing.

PRACTICE: Tell your partner what you appreciate about yourself, about him/her, about life and the planet. Admire and support something that represents competition or jealousy to you about your partner. Admire someone you're jealous of.

4. Brahmacharya *(Moderation)*

This means to direct all of your consciousness towards the development of a higher consciousness. Practice moderation in acts that bring pleasure, such as sexual relations with a loved one, something that is based on healing, and eating food that is nourishing. The goal is not to detract from the higher consciousness.

PRACTICE: Tell each other about the areas in your life that you can improve upon by doing so with moderation and pleasure. Make a list of the things in your life that need positive change. Begin to practice a single moderation each week.

5. Aparigraha *(Greedlessness)*

Let go of the unnecessary things that lead to pleasure. Let go of all the new toys you think you need to make you happy, the external motivations.

Lead a more simple life. The less you have the more clear you become.

PRACTICE: Let go of unnecessary possessions this week. Each month let go of one thing that doesn't spiritually fulfill your path. List the things that you like for pleasure and for spiritual growth. Practice by letting go of a television program this week.

NIYAMAS *(Observances)*

To cultivate a daily routine and a positive approach to life, honor your priorities and free time for yourself. Bring focus and observation to the daily mind.

- THE FIVE NIYAMAS -

1. Shauca *(Cleanliness)*

This is internal and external purity. When we fill our body with junk food, we are impure. When we fill our mind with negative thoughts, we are impure.

PRACTICE: Find a cleansing kriya form of purification and practice. You can choose colonics, breathing, fasting, silence, liver cleanse, meditation, mantras etc. Think of an exercise you use for purity.

2. Samtosha *(Contentment)*

This is being content with what you have. Being satisfied with what life has gifted you.

PRACTICE: Find areas in your life that you're not content with and work on being more at ease in those areas. Sit in your living room and find happiness with exactly what's there. Be satisfied with what you have. Commit yourself to meditate at least twice a week. Use your discipline.

3. Tapas *(Austerity)*

This is self discipline—willpower. Paying one's dues in order to gain a worldly position is not considered austerity. Removal of rude words and moderating your speech is self-discipline. Practicing patience where needed, such as standing in a bank line and/or abstaining from consuming the office coffee and donuts for snacks.

PRACTICE: Willpower, how can you be strong and truthful? What areas of your life need work? Getting up early? Being on time for work? Letting go of afternoon snacks?

Make a list of all the obstacles in your life that need to be removed. List the areas that need discipline and work toward achieving that.

4. Svadhyaya *(Scripture Studies)*

This is studying the spiritual—having a creative life.

PRACTICE: Read spiritual books, self help books, or just good books or articles in philosophy. Attend a spiritual lecture once a month or listen to an enlightening CD. Do any one or a combination of these that allows you to feel your higher power.

5. Ishvara-Pranidhana *(Devotion to God)*

This means seeing the God in all of us. We are God and need to be respecting the divine in ourselves and others—putting God in action.

PRACTICE: Practice loving your neighbor by not talking negatively about them or judging them. See the God in them and love this God. Reach out to a neighbor that you've had negative interludes with. Reach out for peace.

- PRACTICE CONTINUED -

1)   REFLECTION: No partner needed. Sit and reflect on your childhood experiences and list what you think was traumatic and caused you pain. Write about what feelings you had to bury because of the moment.

2)   SOFT FLUIDITY: No partner needed. Lying down with your knees bent, begin to rotate your pelvis in circles, while breathing in through the nose and out through the mouth. Keep moving your pelvis. Observe what feelings surface.

3)   THRUSTING PELVIS: No partner needed. Lie down with

your knees bent and breathe in through the nose and exhale through the mouth. Lift the pelvis slightly as you exhale and , when you inhale, go back down. Do this in increments of 20 lifts.

4)   SHAKE OUT: No partner needed. Stand and begin to shake out all the parts of your body, shake a leg, an arm, your booty. Keep shaking until you've shaken all the defenses and armor away. Later, tell your partner a new boundary that you're creating for yourself.

5)   LET GO OF CONTROL: No partner needed. In a standing position, swing from side to side like a rag doll. Let your arms flap to the sides of your body. Breathe in and out through the mouth. NOTE: It's important to inhale and exhale through the mouth deeply, slowly and completely. Do this for 5 minutes.

6)   APPRECIATE: No partner needed. Approach three people today and tell them something you appreciate about them. Approach three people next week and give them a compliment.

7)   LIONS PUSH AND PULL: Partner necessary. Stand across from your partner with your palms to their palms. Begin to push and pull with and without resistance. Then, push and pull adding sound. For variety, place hands on chest of partner, resist and push away.

8)   CONTENT MOMENT: Partner necessary. One person sits with legs crossed on the floor and the other sits along side of them, placing a hand on the center of the upper back and another on the chest of the person receiving. Receiver closes their eyes and breathes in through the nose and out through the mouth. Giver, for 10 minutes, support this person's breathing with your touch. Keep pressure between your hands and their body. Giver, use phrases such as; "that's it," "let it go," "everything's okay," and so on. Use the supportive phrases to enhance the connection and their release. At the end of the 10 minutes, Giver, cradle this person as if they were a baby. Lie them down and walk away for a moment. Then, return and share your experience.

9)   VULNERABLE MOMENT: Partner necessary. Sit across on the floor from your partner and focus yourself to look into this person's

eyes, expressing a vulnerable moment. Reveal something about yourself to your partner. Express to your partner your fears, boundaries and desires about the relationship and about life.

10)   HAND DANCE: Partner necessary. Begin by making eye contact with someone and take your hands, without touching, move them around in each other's space, begin by mirroring and then see where it goes. Dance the hands along with your partner.

11)   PARTNER COMMUNICATION: Partner necessary. Sit across on the floor or on a chair from each other. Here are a few questions to exchange. One listens and the other talks, then vice versa. At the end, thank each other for sharing.

- *Tell this person what you dislike and like about yourself.*
- *What makes you defensive and on edge? What makes you flowing and open?*
- *What are you noticing in your body? Where do you feel you might be stuck?*
- *What re-occurring problems have you had in your relationship?*
- *What do you want for yourself and for your relationship?*
- *What can you do to help yourself this week?*

12)   BIOENERGETICS: No partner needed. Sit on the floor with legs crossed and interlace hands behind your head, inhale with head under and exhale out the mouth as you bring the neck upwards. The spine will flex and extend. Do for 10 minutes. Bring consciousness to the eyes and imagine the breath moving out from here.

13)   THE TALKER: Partner necessary. You and your partner sit across from each other and start talking back and forth to each other, not hearing what the other person is saying. Then, one at a time talks while the other uses internal focus to listen, then switch. Learn to hear each other from the heart.

14)   TRUST: Group necessary. Form a circle with one person in the center. All the rest form the circle around the one in the center. Center person closes their eyes and is passed around by the other members. The center person is swayed back and forth and being caught from each side. Everyone keep as quiet as possible.

15)   MIRROR MANTRAS: No partner needed. These are statements for you to recite as you stand facing your mirror either aloud or under your breath:

- *"I am strong, nothing steps in my way."*
- *"I am better than you."*
- *"I can do anything."*
- *"I have no fear."*
- *"I am me."*
- *"When I rise to my higher power, I become stronger and enlightened."*
- *"I have the willpower to eat properly."*
- *"I can let go of trivial things and regain my power."*
- *"My senses guide me into believing myself."*
- *"I have gained willpower because I stepped beyond my edge to gain more insight into life."*

You can replace these with your own sayings. You can say a negative and then back it up with a positive statement such as

- *"I am a lonely nothing."*
- *"It's ok for me to accept those feelings of a lonely nothing."*
- *"I can connect with people and be something."*

"In all things, be true to yourself." – *Anonymous*

CHAPTER 9

༄༅

Kinepathics Approach
The Impulsive Self

Breath Alive

We are conceived and born in a breath. At the height of physical pleasure when our breath is taken away, to the structured breathing that helps a woman through labor and delivery. For most, breathing is a natural activity that is not thought about. However, one study indicates that nearly 60% of all emergency transport in the United States is due to breathing disorders ranging from hyperventilation to varying degrees of asthma. This just tells us that breathing is one of the most important aspects of life. "When we learn to breathe properly, we learn to live properly." Once we understand this truth, we learn about prana, which is the life force, and Shakti, which is the presence of the life force. Since the breath is something that we cannot see, it can be considered illusory. How can the breath be so important and us not be aware of it? By being aware of, as well as in contact with your breath, we realize that it is crucial in everything that we do.

According to Dr. Wilhelm Reich, if you breathe poorly, somewhere along the line, important and often harmful emotions weren't expressed, allowing for armor and defenses to be created for survival. Breathing is closely tied to one's emotions so that the more emotional stimulation one has, the more expansive their breath is.

Insufficient breathing is often marked by tension in your diaphragm, giving you the feeling that your chest is tight and uncomfortable. If you were to observe this in someone, you would see that their stomach muscles contract when they inhale.

When we are under stress, we have a tendency to hyperventilate, which is just breathing too quickly. This type of breathing reduces the carbon dioxide and oxygen balance, restricting the arteries going to the brain. When we breathe in and out from the mouth, we charge the breath so that when we let it out, it causes an emotional release—most often of something we didn't even realize was bothering us. When we cry, we breathe through the mouth. This type of breathing activates the orgone energy.

When we breathe through the nose, it helps to sustain the energy charge which enhances sexual control. This way of breathing is best, especially when sleeping since toxins filter out through the hairs in the nose. Breathing through the nose also sustains the balance of oxygen and carbon dioxide. When you are able to breathe expansively, (deeply, filling the lungs), sexual enjoyment is greater. This alone should motivate you to breathe deeply and be aware of it.

Proper breathing is something that you need to re-learn if you want to attain your highest goals and live life to your fullest potential. Life begins with breath. One thing you will notice is that this type of breathing is work, just like aerobics or jogging. How much of your breath can you summon and have in the moment? When we breathe, we open up, becoming more alive, realizing the many dimensions that make up who we are. Of course, we know that we are breathing daily, but are you aware of how affective your breathing is? Breathing supports thoughts, emotions, movements, and overall energy in the world.

In order to increase your life force, you must attain and sustain healthy breathing. This helps to maintain the flame of life within all of us. Proper breathing both increases and teaches us about our passions. Our passions are closely tied with our emotions. Babies breathe massively until they get caught up in the constraints of the world. Our bodies forget how to breathe deeply, so we have to re-learn it, thus awakening our primal animal, which keeps the body from living patterns that are not our own.

How we relate in life is dependent on how we breathe. Breathing directs our movements, focus, gestures and intuition. The more we breathe, the more we appreciate the things that have an impact on our lives such as weather, becoming successful in our chosen field, keeping fit, and building healthier relationships.

Breathing needs acknowledgement because it not only supports the body's movement, it aligns our emotions for spiritual development. Relationships that are built today all tend to suffer for many reasons. I believe that one of these reasons is due to improper breathing, because this causes the life force to suffer. When we breathe improperly, we are cutting off oxygen to areas of the body and the mind that rely on that element in order to function properly. Some of us are cut off from the pelvic energy—the foundation of the life force. Others tend to cut out the energy at the chest, sabotaging the language of the heart.

When we breathe properly, we openly distribute energy to the areas of the body that require love, attention, and liberation. Breathing invites others to become present in your world. When we become sexually excited, our breathing increases naturally. When we breathe wildly, the physical pleasures heighten, becoming temporarily out of control. In order to prolong these sensations and expand on each session of lovemaking, there are different breathing techniques you can try to help distribute more sexual energy throughout the body.

There are many types of breathing exercises with which to practice. I have outlined four different ones that you can pick and choose from. You may even wish to interchange them. We will learn the following four breathing exercises: Orgone, Breath of Fire, Animal, and Fire Orgasm.

- NOTES -

Orgone Energy Breath (Release)

This breathing technique is a transformational, emotional release exercise. It is practiced by inhaling and exhaling through the mouth, using long deep breaths, as if through a straw from the chest to the stomach. It is accompanied with bio-energetic exercises as developed by Dr. Alexander Lowen. The breathing was invented by Dr. Wilhelm Reich who discovered that emotional disorders severely disturbed natural breathing patterns. He also noted that everything is affected by breathing. When these patterns are restored to a natural pulsation, breathing becomes natural again.

This type of breathing activates the chakras which are the energy systems of the body. By building an energy charge through breathing, we discovered it helps with the release of body armor that stays hidden in the muscles. You will find this to be a profound deepening of your subconscious mind. During the practice of these breathing exercises, the charge engages the armor which, together, releases unhealed trauma. Emotions become challenged, rising to the surface. We do this to open the passageway and make room for love. Remember, that this breathing is done by completely inhaling and exhaling through the mouth. By doing this, you open and expand the connective tissue more. This breathing exercise focuses on opening the different segments of the body. It begins with your eyes and works its way down the body.

Breath of Fire (Recharge)

The Kundalini energy sits at the base of the spine, (tail bone) and is also called the "coiled energy." This energy is the breath of fire and sits at the Muladhara, the first chakra, which is the root center of the anus. This breathing exercise is a cleansing breath that clears the toxins, while oxygenating the blood stream. It restores the body's natural heat. It also causes powerful detoxification and is done by inhaling and exhaling briskly through the nose, resulting in increased lung capacity. The mouth remains closed, lips are sealed. This powerful detoxification tool causes an awareness of the pulses of your diaphragm. By increasing lung capacity, you strengthen your nervous system which, over time, increases confidence and imparts courage. This particular exercise is the most profound breathing used to awaken and restore your Kundalini energy. It is referred to as a power breath and is accompanied with body motion. This breathing exercise can be practiced alone or with a partner and is generally done with the body in some kind of motion, particularly the spine.

Animal Breath (Dynamic)

This exercise involves breathing from the open mouth and throat. It is similar to the la maz and Tarzan breaths. This exercise involves pulsing, using short breaths from your stomach, while making sounds as you exhale. Begin by puckering your lips then, move the lips in and out, making wind sounds as you blow out. Next, you shift to the throat, making sound from there while connecting the energy to the lip movements. While panting from the stomach, through the throat, add sounds from your throat such as "HA." Do this in incremental pauses with your stomach. Put your hand on your stomach and feel it pulse as you breathe. This breathing flows through your connective tissue, spinal fluid and entire musculoskeletal system, creating more space in the body. During labor and delivery, this breathing eases the pain and makes room for the fetus to move through the birth canal. This exercise is good to do alone and/or with a partner. Dynamic breathing is accompanied with fluid undulating movements.

Fire Orgsam Breath (Energy)

This type of breathing will produce warmth all throughout and around the body. It also helps you to achieve the full body orgasm—the heightened pleasure of life. This complete experience, while intensely pleasurable, also helps to transmute energy. Inhale through the nose while contracting the perineum muscles in the lower pelvic floor or anus (Kegels). Then, while breathing, pull the energy up from the genitals to the third eye (the forehead area). This stimulates the emotions and increases sensations. This is best practiced with a partner in the Yab Yum position. Breathe in through the nose and exhale through the mouth. While inhaling, relax the Kegels and on exhale squeeze. (Contract)

Decrease Fears, Defenses

A lot of us experience anxiety and fear due to the stresses of life. The key is to recognize it and let it go. No one has to live with anxiety. It's a false part of your innate being that doesn't belong to you. Anxiety eats away at our lives. What is anxiety and how do we get it? Anxiety has to do with strong emotion. It is a combination of fear, apprehension and worry and is often accompanied by physical sensations such as heart palpations, nausea, chest pain, and shortness of breath. When the emotions are unbalanced, anxiety occurs. The goal is to balance out the emotional self so that we don't overextend our energy and love so that we don't stray from who we are. Anxiety can also be associated with sadness as well as happiness, closely tied to our instinct for survival—the fight or flight principle.

Anxiety is often triggered by any situation that involves a decision or judgment, no matter how slight. Paul Tillich, the theologian, characterized anxiety as "The trauma of non-being." Sometimes anxiety can make us feel as if we are about to die. Another association includes obsessive thinking. Reflect back to your upbringing. Was there a balance of parental love given to you? Were your parents both there? Did they extend touch to you? Did they show their emotions around you? If parents are uptight about expressing their emotions, chances are good that children grow up either overly emotional and needy, or just the opposite; holding onto every ounce of attention they receive.

When we excessively use our energy, we are overextending a part of our self that was not loved. So, we usually do too much, either to try and fill the void, or to get back what we lost. It's a vicious cycle and can go on forever. Usually the person that overextends tends to attract a person who is uptight and full of anxiety. Anxiety comes from expressing, also from over expressing. In relationships, the one who overextends can end up hurt in the end, experiencing obsession, while the one that holds on, also experiences anxiety from the pressure of having to open up to it all. There are ways to help each other manage and maintain this. Those who bury their anxiety are usually affected in every part of their personal lives, including the sexual. When your emotions are in balance and you have clarity, everything else just falls into place, including heightened sensations. Allow me to show you the ways of clearing the path of anxiety, so that you can lead a healthier lifestyle.

Developing Trust

Trust is about awareness. It's about your inner peace, that space you call love. In order to trust, you must go deep inside yourself, creating an inner world of awareness where you can retreat when you feel lost. Mistrust is a feeling of loss, a feeling of emptiness—of no connection. When we trust, we open our hearts to a greater degree of love. To trust is to let down your barriers and look inside yourself. Take a moment to reflect on the most sacred time of your past. Take a moment to see yourself as a child. Your parents are there and you trust them because they are your parents. Trust is the knowledge that everything is okay inside— that whatever is there is supposed to be there. When you trust, it is a moment in truth. You can trust again when you forgive your heart. When we trust our thoughts and actions, it makes it alright to trust the world.

Developing a Spontaneous Self

The moment of spark in your heart allows you to unwind and reach out of the darkness, going to that far away place. That place is called connection. When we are spontaneous, we understand our truth at its deepest level. We understand the level of commitment it takes to be our self. It is a sense of awareness in allowing you to be just that—for the moment—to be innate and go forth with inherent instincts. Spontaneity is being in the truth of the moment, the heart of the soul and the light of the day. Allow yourself to go forth and seek, without thinking; you can delve for just that moment. It is the raw immediacy of your action. To be spontaneous, both the body and the mind need to be loose. Spontaneity is the private moment of life that we actually strive for and surrender to. It is the newness, liveliness, and freshness of your heart.

- PRACTICE -

Orgone Energy Breath

1)   INITIATION BREATH: No partner needed. Begin by lying flat on your back with your knees bent and your feet flat on the floor. Close your eyes and consciously breathe in and out through your mouth. NOTE: This is not nasal breathing. Do this for 5 minutes and stop. Then repeat. Continue this for 20 minutes. Place one hand on your chest and the other on your stomach. This is a wonderful breathing exercise to practice weekly. Be sure to connect the stomach to the chest breath.

2)   REACH OUT: Partner necessary. Face your partner, standing with your knees slightly bent. Reach out toward your partner with your hands and arms, making eye contact. In this position, breathe in and out through your mouth. The following are some statements you can say: "I need you, love me, teach me, help me", "I am angry, I want out". Do this off and on for 20 minutes.

Breath of Fire

1)   SEATED AWAKENING: No partner needed. Sit in a crossed legged position with your hands on your knees. Begin the breathing and stomach pulsing. Then, add the flexion and extension of the spine, bending back and forth as you breathe. Make sure your lips are sealed. Breathe in and out your nose with energy.

2)   OPPOSITION: No partner needed. Lie on your back with your legs at a 90 degree angle. Take your right hand and reach up toward the left leg and vice versa. Do this about 10 to 20 times with the breathing. Your legs are in opposition. Breathe in and out your nose with energy. Your lips should be sealed.

3)   PARTNER SUPPORT: Partner necessary. Stand behind your partner. While your partner breathes in and out through the nose forcefully, moving the pelvis and spine asymmetrically in a fluid dance, place your fingers along their spine to encourage chakra vibrations and support their breathing and movement.

Animal Breath

1)   SEATED SPIRAL: No partner needed. Sit in a crossed legged position with your hands on your knees. Begin breathing while rotating in a circular pattern from the ribs around from side to side. Keep the movements going, changing patterns. Move, curve and spiral around. Continue to breathe intermittently. Pucker the lips and let the breath out and take it in at the throat with your mouth open. Like Hu-Ha with the breath.

2)   WIRED CAT: No partner needed. On all fours, like a cat, begin to move around, spiraling asymmetrically and symmetrically. Do a fluid dance. Find a balance in the movement and breathe intermittently.

Fire Orgasm Breath

1)   PELVIC LIFT: No partner needed. Lie flat on your back with your knees bent. Inhale through the nose and exhale through the mouth. Begin to lift the pelvis toward the sky, exhaling with sound and contracting the perineum area. (Kegels). As you come back down, inhale, relaxing the perineum area and repeat. Practice this every day for 20 minutes at a time.

2)   PING PONG: Partner necessary. Stand, facing your partner. Move your pelvis forward and back. One of you move forward while the other moves backward with the hips like ping pong. When you move forward, contract the perineum, (Kegel.) Breathe in through the nose and out through the mouth. Practice for fun.

"The breath is life. Learn to use it properly and you may live longer with a greater quality of life." –Anita

CHAPTER 10

❧

Kinepathics Approach
The Intuitive Self

The Body, Mind & Sexual Awareness

The moment of truth has arrived or better yet, you have arrived at this moment in time, space, dimension and interlude. Since this is the case, you've been practicing awareness. The mind was first, followed closely by the body as an all inclusive dimension. Now we add the sexual spirit to bring it full circle with force. I call it *Tantra Wisdom*™ *technique.*

When we realize that the soul reveals itself to the planet through our senses, it is a gentle awakening. It becomes a fluid nature — this water of light that floats and joins the duration of a mere second in time. Why do we hesitate and forget who we are? Why do we imagine that the life force is in some other world, when it exists in this world? — The world of capture and the force of flow.

It is this mind, body and spirit connection that opens our eyes to the world as we really see it. It is only an illusion that blinds our awareness, ultimately blinding us to our own sexual suppression — sexpression. When we understand that we are but one in a world of one-ness, we will have evolved beyond the separation of the truth. Having a sensual experience is not only about sex, but to look at a beautiful painting — the art in nature, the beauty in everything.

"Movement is the most transformative way into the real self."
– Willem Dafoe, Actor

- NOTES -

Unlock Yourself

Part of letting go sometimes requires an actual physical release. Your body is like a warehouse that stores any and all trauma you've ever experienced. Part of unlocking the body is letting go of the rigid tension that creates stress and inhabits the body's natural organism. Once the body is set free, the mind becomes liberated and you will be able to accept life for what it is. You will be able to live more freely.

The body image is formed according to what you experienced in childhood. If you were exposed to fear, you may have shallow breathing habits, not getting enough oxygen into your system. This type of breathing is called chest breathing. If you were left alone, you may be dealing with abandonment issues, leaving you to feel that your body is restricted in certain areas—disconnected.

When the rib cage is tense, it constricts your breathing, making it difficult to get a full breath. It is because your connective tissue is not living. This decreases one's lack of vitality, thus your quality of life. As a child, we are free and thrive from every impulse—every challenge. As time goes on, our natural instincts become closed off. We begin locking ourselves away from the world from the approximate age of nine. Getting back to our natural instincts is a part of healing and unlocking the self.

Sexual Energy Aliveness

Sexual energy is the most repressed energy of all, and is due to governmental, religious, and corporate developments that work to keep this most sacred of energies repressed. Sexual energy is part of the body-mind connection and should come full circle with such. First the mind, then the body kept it all together. Now it is the sexual energy that does. This powerful energy cannot be separated from the spectrum that activates and animates our consciousness. Sexual energy is an expression that keeps us innately connecting and merging with the human animal. It is the way of life.

In the array of giving and receiving, sexual energy is our true power. This energy has proven to be more powerful than the heart. If sexual energy is accepted easier than the heart, sex becomes one with the physical mind. Sexual energy is the expression of fullness. It is the energy that teaches us what life is and becomes our guide through it. This energy does not sit or work alone; rather it needs to function from our whole being in order for our truth and identity to be recognized. Sexual energy is repressed because of its hidden powers. If not opened, accepted, and channeled properly, it can redirect itself toward all kinds of violence.

When we are sexually alive, it is hard to be manipulated by others. We are primal animals. Feeding off each other is what we do. When our sexual energy is alive and existing in its own instinctual way, we can do anything. This energy has power because it is the love found throughout the body.

"The orgasm is no longer a mere biological function used in procreation, nor the side effect of casual pleasure. It is the very center of the human experience and ultimately determines the happiness of the human race"
–Wilhelm Reich

Sexual Heart

It takes a lot of love to survive. If you want to be rich, you need cultivation. The wealth of your sexual energy lies within your heart. When the heart and sex chakra merge, the world, literally, opens for you. Your sex is in your heart and vice versa. When we have sex without heart, the heart ages, it armors, causing it to work against its will to continue living. You might not feel it right away, but later it builds, becoming stress, anxiety, negative thinking, etc. One can be love even without being in love. The abundance of your power is within your sexual energy. When this energy is abused, you lose that wonderful wealth. People, who abuse their sexual nature, go against the force within. When we abuse ourselves sexually, we lose our worth. We become poor and wasted. But, if we harness this sacred energy, we cultivate great power. The heart naturally responds to this rich treasure. Surprisingly, it's the mind that gets in the way. The heart has a different language from the mind, so when these two come together harmoniously, there is peace. Sometimes they fight each other because of the separation that was once there. The brain is also in the body, so there are brain cells throughout our physical selves.

Sustaining Energy (Bandhas)

Bandhas are energy locks (valves) for the use of penetrating and activating the body energy. These valves lock the fire energy, the heat that is created from breathing and contractions within. It is this heat that keeps passion alive. There are three bandhas in the body. They are the: Jalandhara lock located in the neck or chin, the Uddiyana lock, located in the abdomen, and the Moola, which is located in the naval floor. When you execute a bandha, you lock certain areas of the pelvis. Maha bandhas require a successive engagement of Jalandhara, Uddiyana, and Moola Bandha. When you do this, you bring the entire body into focus. It affects the hormonal secretions of the pineal gland and regulates the entire endocrine system. Bandha comes from India.

Using bandhas also soothes anger. Moola bandha develops out of Uddiyana. The three main muscles involved in the three bandhas are the perineal, abdominal, and cervical. Practiced contraction of these muscles affects the nervous, circulatory, respiratory, endocrine and the energy systems (chakras.) When a muscle is contracted, a nerve impulse is relayed to the brain which triggers the neural circuits and nervous centers, affecting our state of consciousness as the brain makes the necessary adjustments.

The performance of bandhas leads to a general massaging effect of the muscles and internal organs. Physically, the bandhas harmonize the efficient functioning of the endocrine system. Bandhas regulate the biorhythms in the body, stabilize the menstrual periods, lower blood pressure, lower heart rate, and reorder confused and or crossed neural circuits in the brain. This serves to retrain our brain.

Bandhas redirect the power of a dam wall. They are not only locks, but removers of locks and blockages in the form of physical and mental impurities. When we experience tension and fear, respiration becomes short and shallow, but when relaxed, the breaths are longer and deeper. Bandhas empty the body of rubbish, toxins and intensify the Pranayama process in ridding the body of waste.

Jalandhara Bandha

This particular bandha (cervical contraction), is known as a chin lock. Press your chin against your chest with your eyes closed and retain your breathing, either after exhalation or inhalation. This exercise has tremendous effects on the heart, lungs, brain, concentration center and the eyes. It also affects the pituitary and pineal glands. With the forward flexion of the chin, our thyroid and thymus glands are also affected.

Uddiyana Bandha

This bandha (abdominal contraction), is a complete exhalation followed by a deep contraction of your abdominal muscles. A profound mudra when combined, can overcome any and all digestive problems. This bandha compresses the digestive organs, adrenal glands, kidneys, and most important, the solar plexus. This is the "brain in the stomach" which is squeezed, returning a flood of energy that is generated in the abdomen and chest. This bandha has healing qualities. It also tones the sympathetic nervous system, encouraging it to work more efficiently.

Moola Bandha

This bandha (perineal contraction), deals with the rectum, anus, and the sphincter lock controls by regulating your breathing either in exhalation or inhalation, with retention of your breath.

The Moola bandha is the most effective way to strengthen your pelvic floor muscles which are needed for sustaining sexual energy, intensifying climactic sensations, and controlling other sensations which benefit men who experience premature ejaculation.

Moola bandha is used to awaken the root chakra and vajroli sahajoli mudra and ashwini mudras are used for awakening the swadhisthana, or (naval) chakra. It also helps women hold the male organ in their yoni for a longer time. These muscles need to be trained like any other muscle in the body. Moola bandha is practiced only on inhalation during intercourse. In yoga, it is practiced on both inhalation and exhalation. This contraction stimulates both the sensory-motor and autonomic nervous systems within the pelvic region. When the moola bandha is performed, pelvic stimulation activates parasympathetic fibers that emerge from the neck and pelvic areas. The sympathetic fibers emerge from the upper and lower back areas.

Maha Bandha (The Great Lock)

This is the fourth bandha and is a combination of the other three. This is why it is called "great," because it's more of a comprehensive body contraction.

The Concept of Lock

The meaning of bandha is paradoxical. When the body locks, or contracts, on a physical level, a subtle process of unlocking goes on at the same time on the mental and pranic levels. Bandhas allow the body to regain physical and mental relaxation. To remove the tension in the body, we must first exaggerate it by voluntary contractions in the muscles. Bandhas affect the physical, pranic, mental, psychic and causal bodies. They are associated with energy centers in the spine and brain. Bandhas are more dynamic, explosive and immediate in effect than a simple contraction of the legs or arms.

Pubococcygeus Muscle (Love Muscle)

This muscle controls your bladder. It's a large muscle that goes around the anus and most of the pelvic floor. In women, the muscle fibers circle the vagina, and in men they pass under the prostate gland. The pelvic control (PC) muscle supports the organs nestled in the pelvis, prevents incontinence, and increases sexual pleasure for both men and women. Over time, the exercises tone the vagina and allow for a more satisfying orgasm. Many men who have trained their love muscle find that it allows them to delay orgasm as well as prevent premature ejaculation. Men have claimed that they can have two or more orgasms in a row without needing a rest in between. The PC muscle stimulates blood flow, develops endurance, and increases orgasmic intensity and sexual control.

Perineum - Perineal Body

These are the muscles in and around the vagina and urinary opening that help support the uterus (womb), bladder, and rectum in women. In men, they are between the anus/rosebud and scrotum. The PC muscles are part of this whole pelvic floor area on both men and women. It is considered the second G spot in men. Perineal muscles can become weakened by a number of factors, such as; childbirth, decreased estrogen levels during and following menopause, and increased pressure on the muscles. Strengthening this area tones the sexual area, helps to sustain climax, and builds an inner confidence and authentic power. The muscles of the perineum are divided into two groups; those of the anal region and of the urogenital region. A strong perineum helps us gain greater control over such processes as urination, defecation and sexual intercourse.

Connective Fascia Tissue (CFT)

What part do contractions play in helping the body sustain the heat of energy? Proper breathing, along with contractions, holds the energy inside. Breathing expansively creates the heat and the bandha, (contraction,) is the valve that seals it in. This heat that builds up within the body loosens the connective tissue, making the body more liberated, trusted as well as flexible—hot.

Connective fascia tissue, or CFT, is gelatinous in nature, needing to move in order to remain living. The nature of this tissue mediates the aging process. The body consists of various types of cells. The brain, nerves, muscles, and organs all have different cells. Then there are connective tissue cells. This tissue is the fluid, agile, mobile tissue of the body. It has many shapes and sizes. Bone, cartilage and red blood cells are also forms of connective tissue. All the cells are held within the fascia.

The body structure is held up not by the bones, but rather the fascia and its' tensile strength; because the fascia has the ability to be anywhere in the body due to its fluid nature. It is very important that we nourish and maintain this tissue, because the body would literally fall apart if it weren't for fascia. Fascia is referred to as the connective tissue proper. It is a container, revolving around the fluid nature in the body, creating boundaries in order to contain the body's liquids.

Contractions on the pelvic floor strengthen the fascia and surrounding muscle, thus developing strong pelvic muscles. By strengthening this area, the body becomes richer in nature. The fascia was among the first cells to be developed at birth, since the heart and brain needed a cushioned container to stay in place safely.

During the PC contraction we are contracting the muscle surrounded by the fascia. Fascia creates the 'cables' that provide the lift and movement. This amazing tissue is like a spider web that connects and travels throughout the entire body. The more the fascia is stimulated and strengthened, the more flexible the body becomes and the better quality of life you will have. Healthy fascia promotes a mind of freedom and clarity. The more heat sustained, the more disciplined you are toward love, and the more focused you are on prolonging the pleasures of life. The best exercise for fascia is primal undulation. In this way, the muscle and fascia work together.

Primal Fluid Undulations

The primal is part of your being and body that is instinctual. The way we move affects the way we think. Your body and breath move in waves of motion.

Gestures are "thoughted motions." Gestures take the place of words and can be as oppressive and hurtful toward others as any spoken or unspoken negative thought. However, they can also be warming and nourishing. Gesturing comes from our primal self.

If you have ever watched animals, they are very instinctual, gesturing with their paws and facial expressions through their natural body. We love them so because they don't think. In a world where we wear more than one hat, so-to-speak, we work toward dissolving, or rather integrating the body, mind and sexual self so that we can be liberal, reverting back to our simpler, yet instinctual nature of God.

Undulation allows us to free ourselves from our self-imposed bondage while still living in the world. Our bodies are mostly made up of water. We are like this wave living on land that frees us from the confines of life's obstacles. The fluid body is the environment from which we surface. It is this environment that we must harness and nourish. Everyone can benefit from pelvic healing.

Fluidity is the ability and mutability to change shape, form and structure. When we are in touch with our fluid selves, we enable expression to every arc, spiral and curve that we perform. The fluid self consists of undulations, gyrations, curves, arcs, and spirals. I discovered the fluid system when my CFT opened up as in a form of physical communication of healing when I was a sick child. As you've read, this actually saved me. Had I not done this, I would not have survived.

Attaining the fluid state is easy, since flowing is a growth system that stretches beyond the body's natural defenses. It is a movement that is inherent, allowing for a sensual feeling. Undulation combines the emotions, balancing out your feelings to love. Years of built up anger is unhealthy in that it inhibits and stagnates the fluid energy thereby, shutting down the pathways of the body's vital communication system. To exercise from your fluid self includes all the elements of gravity, your emotions and the physical and spiritual self.

Chi is a vital part of the fluid system; an energy form. Chi energy regulates movement in the body, engaging the autonomic system. The body is drawn to its inner gorge, thus recreating from different levels of perception. The body is an artistic mastery in itself, a mystery to you. Changes happen involuntarily, just like everyday things happen in life. Our natural fluidity is bombarded by structure. The natural flow of human-ness is the fluid system we know is hidden within us. The body is a fertile field, yielding huge crops when properly tended. Fluidity is something that, sometimes we can feel, and yet we are afraid to go there. Being tuned to your fluid nature opens you so that you can become innovatively creative. The idea is to flow with your own energy and not someone else's. When we are in motion using our fluidity, our emotions make a connection, thus creating energy, thought and centered-ness.

There are many different types of fluid in the body. There is the lymph, synovial, blood and cerebrospinal fluid or CSF. Lymph and CSF are similar. Lymph flows toward the center of the body, while CSF is a centrally produced fluid that cushions the brain. Synovial fluid is lubrication that can be found around the joints—the lubrication fluid system. All the fluids of the body meet, supporting the spaces inside from head to toe.

Synovial is the freedom fluid, since when the joints are lubricated, the body is able to relax, spread, and shake. Fluids are combinable in one's abilities just as emotions are. The parts of the body where the fluids are located are the areas of statements. The lymph node fluid needs the synovial fluid to express. Lymph fluid sits at the groin, under the arms, in areas where it often goes unexpressed. Synovial joint action directs the fluids to become one.

Blood is similar to emotion. It's thick, yet full, and has a flow that enables full integration with your feelings. Together the body personality can experience dynamic direction along with the sensual foreground. The more we connect and move our fluids, the more adaptable our personality when changes are experienced.

When we ride or become parasitic on another's energy, it's because we have not yet found our identity. Shifting the necessary power comes from a strong emotional foundation. We are drawn into conflicting situations because, internally and emotionally, we are searching for something outside of the self. When this happens, it is best to fully exercise, moving fluidly until shifts become internalized. Shifting brings us to consciousness, which allows you to use your sexual power to abort interruptions from the flow of your true identity. Fluidity is the available inner strength that expands the concepts of one's own resources.

The fluid energy is very empowering to the self. Chi is the center of gravity which exists and hovers at the pelvic level of the body, otherwise known as the core. Your chi is part of your fluid energy. This energy center is responsible for generating fluid throughout the body. Being fluid opens us to everything, the true love of the self and elimination of your defenses and boundaries. The more boundaries with which we feel the need to live, the less in flow we are with our fluid self. Fluid is what you are. When you get there, you'll see. Fluids provide the safest place to be on the planet. We came from a fluid-safe womb. If it had been up to us, we probably would have remained there. The fluid directs our consciousness so that when our inner thoughts reach our brain, we freely give ourselves the permission to let go. The fluid system is part of the emotional based self. In movement, there is stillness and in stillness, there is movement. Fluidity is part of the expansive world.

Touch and Isolation

How important is touch to you? Without touch, babies don't survive. Are you the isolated inward type who is afraid to show emotion? Are you the type to have sex with your partner and not ask him/her for the touch you need afterward? Reflect on how much touch you received while growing up. Were you sexually or physically abused so that you fear touch? Do you allow yourself to receive loving touch massages? Hugging is a wonderful part of life. Hugging with boundaries is healthy. Do you hug people when you see them? Touch stimulates the cells and keeps the body connected to trust.

Touch breaks isolation and stimulates the senses. Feeling isolated can be a result of living with fear. Touch is a step in the right direction to reduce the body armor and open your heart to a deeper level of love. Touch can give you courage to seek the truth. Give yourself the permission to open up and show us your soul. Isolation is you looking at the world and the world looking at you. Make a connection.

- PRACTICE -

1)   MOOLA BANDHA: No partner needed. Sit in a comfortable position. Place your tongue to the roof of your mouth and inhale in through your nose and exhale out the mouth, through the teeth(make a smile). Feel a sense of pulling the energy up. On inhalation, press the sphincter muscle outward, and on the exhalation, squeeze the entire pelvic floor musculature. Continue to repeat this process of muscle tension and relaxation at least eight times. This is Moola Bandha and should be performed twice a day in the early morning and/or the evening.

2)   KEGELS: No partner needed. In order to recognize this muscle, start by urinating, then stopping the flow of urine. If you can do this, you can control and strengthen the pelvic flow. Tighten the muscle for two to three seconds then, relax. Repeat. Next tighten the muscle and release five times as quickly as you can. Practice each Kegel exercise at least 50 to 100 times a day. This is one exercise you can do anywhere and anytime. This will greatly increase blood flow and awareness of sensations throughout the whole body.

3)   ELBOW THRUST: No partner needed. This is done from a standing position with your knees slightly bent. Begin breathing deeply in and out through your mouth. Thrust your right elbow back as if you're

pushing someone away then, do the other side. Keep doing this for 10 minutes. Inhale on one side and exhale on the other. As you continue, add "Ha" sounds to your elbow thrusts. Add phrases like "move out of my way." You may want to add phrases of positive affirmations of inner strength.

4)   SHAKE OUT: No partner needed. To stimulate the connective fascia, stand comfortably and begin to shake yourself lightly. Begin shaking your hands over your head then, to your sides. Shake one leg then the other. Shake your whole body until you feel charged. Shake out any pain, fear and anger. Shake your booty.

5)   SIDE LEGS: No partner needed. Lie on your side and raise your top leg and begin to let it float in the space as if it's the first time it has moved. Feel the suspension, dancing from an involuntary place of love. Switch sides. Utilize Velcro weights if available and you are able.

6)   SUSPENSION LEGS: No partner needed. Stand with one side of your body against the wall pushing and resisting with one hand as if pushing the wall away from you. On the free side of your body, begin to lift your leg in balance and suspend, dance the leg away from the body in an asymmetrical fashion. Move it around from the waist, sending the energy down the leg from your ribs. Switch sides.

7)   CAT MOVEMENT MEDITATIONS: No partner needed. Get down on your hands and knees in a yoga cat position. Begin moving your spine up and down then, around while remaining in the cat pose. Change movements between asymmetrical and symmetrical. Continue moving in and around the space breathing in and out through your mouth.

8)   PELVIC DANCE: No partner needed. Standing in front of the mirror, begin moving your pelvis in circles and then any way that feels right. Change direction. Go around, forward and backward. Do this for 15 minutes to music with a good beat.

9)   CHILD'S POSE: No partner needed. Get down on the floor into a yoga child's pose. Begin moving the spine in, out and around; engage your neck. Connect to the feeling in your spine. Stay in undulated

movement for 10 minutes.

10)   SQUAT: No partner needed. Come to a yoga squat position while breathing in and out of your mouth. Move upward partway with resistance and a "Ha" sound and then back down. Repeat this rhythm of up and down. Feel the armor melt in your legs. Do 3 sets of 10 then, return to a child's pose afterward with knees apart.

11)   STRADDLE: No partner needed. Sit in a straddle yoga position with your legs wide apart. Then, begin to undulate movements from your pelvis, bend the knees, keeping your hands behind you on the floor. Do this for 10 minutes.

12)   KIND TOUCH: Random partners. Touching is very important. Today, touch five people. Shake a hand, touch an arm in conversation, admire their clothing and touch, rub shoulders to make body contact. Lightly touch someone's hair.

13)   BODY CONTACT TOUCH: Partner necessary. This exercise is to break the feeling of isolation. Go near a partner, someone you trust, and stand side by side making arm contact. Balance your feet and lean in toward them then, move away. Connect to the moment of letting go and the point of contact. Feel the moment of letting go. Next face your partner and with palms together, try moving in toward your partner and away, both pushing and pulling away and toward each other.

14)   BEATING THE PILLOWS: No partner needed. Stack a few big pillows. Take a tennis racket or a towel twirled up with tape around it. Get down on your knees. Begin with 10 deep breaths in and out through your mouth. Continue breathing in and out through your mouth. When you're ready, raise your arms over the top of your head. With tennis racket or towel and on inhalation, hit the pillows then, exhale as you come through it. Repeat as necessary until you start to feel your emotions opening. Begin adding statements such as "I hate you." "I'm pissed at you." "Let me go." "I want to be free." Add names and whatever phrases you feel are necessary. Using your imagination, pretend you see the person there whom you want to get out of your system.

15)   TUG OF WAR: Partner necessary. Take a towel and begin a tug of war with your partner. While one pulls one direction, the other pulls the opposite direction. Continue pulling until you feel relief from emotional tension. Add words such as yes/no. One of you says yes, the other, no as you continue the tug of war.

16)   MUSCLE TENSION: No partner needed. This exercise begins by walking around the room, (your living room is fine, but if you have a larger room, that would be better.) As you walk around in different directions, scan the room with your eyes. Begin to tense each muscle in the body. Start with the legs, feet, and toes, moving up the body to the hands, arms, stomach, pelvis, the face and neck. Keep moving around the room as you tense up. Repeat a few times then, release. Add words such as "I feel tense", "its ok for me to feel tense".

17)   PELVIC UNDULATION: Partner necessary. Working with a partner, one of you lies down on your back with your knees bent. (Receiver) Your partner sits beside you. (Giver) The receiver stays flat with the pelvis moving in-between symmetrical and asymmetrical undulations. The giver places their hands on th receiver's pelvic bones, and with gentle pressure, tries holding them down while they move—creating resistance. The receiver moves while the giver applies resistance. Do for 15 minutes.

18)   CHAOTIC MILLING MOVEMENT: No partner needed. Move around the room in a chaotic spin, swirling and moving about. Just let go and allow the moment. Stop and start.

19)   RIB OPEN: Partner necessary. Stand with your partner facing you. One person begins to move their body in any way that feels right. Start by moving the pelvis and ribs around with your eyes closed. Your partner is to place their hands on both sides of your ribs to support or follow your movement.

20)   WILD TONGUE: No partner needed. Sit in a dark, quiet space and begin to move your tongue around the inside and outside of your mouth. Move it as if it's watering for a good meal. Outline the lips and

the teeth and just let it hang out. Allow it to move freely.

21)   NECK UNDULATION: Partner necessary. Sit in a relaxed, easy pose and begin moving your neck in any way that feels comfortable. Your partner is to place their hands on your occipital bone (Large bone at the top of the neck) and the top of your head. Do this to support their movement. Switch between following and leading the movement.

"When you have reached emotional freedom, you have found a treasure beyond price." - *Anonymous*

CHAPTER 11

Kinepathics Approach
The Confused Self

Communication

Without communication, you have confusion and frustration. Being able to communicate well is, what could be, the most important element to human understanding. We take for granted the ability to ask for what we want simply because we can. When we communicate clearly, we open ourselves to the universe with the ability to express the beauty of our soul.

Compassionate communication means communing with honesty and openness to another being. When you neglect your voice, a part of you dies a little each day. Don't be afraid to open your thoughts and feelings by plunging into speaking with your voice. However, when you speak, do it softly and with truth. Project warmth and love in your voice when you speak. Talk to your partner and friends, letting them know how you feel. Let them know who you are. Communication is a key pathway in the right direction to the light.

Share your thoughts and feelings, and not only hear, but listen to what others have to say. Good communication involves listening and hearing each other, bringing about an understanding of one another. The way you say things is a very important, effective part of communication.

When we are born, it is into a sterile, harsh space without words we understand. We find love in a place without words, an aloneness we wish could last for awhile. The good news is; you can reclaim this feeling when you fall in love with someone. When a baby is born, it bonds with its mother through the eyes, and it is in this presence where tantra begins. It is an accepted practice for the parents and peers to use silly words and phrases such as;

"Coochie-coo," "Hi baby," "You're so beautiful," "Look at you," "You're so adorable," etc. It is these loving, affectionate words that become an important part of the *existing compassion* we carry throughout our lives.

We show and feel emotional compassion toward our babies and continue through the many subsequent years to come. Later, when the child learns words, the affectionate presence that once was so strong, has changed. We can only hope that our affections and loving words are conditioned in this still new, present child. It's the conditioning in the body that the baby learns and understands first. This emotional nourishment feeds the nervous system. Without communication you have confusion and frustration.

- NOTES -

Developing Respectful Communication

Communication is a powerful art form in life that stems from the heart and not the ego. When we strengthen our communication skills, we delve into a whole other side of the self. Pay close attention to the way you communicate with someone. Do you use a non-violent tone? Are the words compassionate? When we use that soft, caring tone, it comes from the truth, and when we have mastered it, good communication becomes richly fueled with truth, passion, love and respect. Speak clearly and concisely in order to understand each other better. By interjecting different subjects into conversations, for discussion, where there are others present, is a wonderful way of learning. Let go of the denial in your thoughts — the shame in the moment, and allow the words to come alive.

Developing Clarity

As we bring clarity to our strengths, we bring clarity to our minds. In order for one to find stability, balance, power, sexuality/sensuality, heart connections, the mind (ajna chakra), must be open and clear, first and foremost. Clarity is the most important understanding of structure. To be free, you must have clarity. The objective of clarity is to be free of negativity, distraction and obstruction. When your senses are clear, you will attract less negativity. Clarity also raises consciousness, thus raising the body energy. Ego and breath both play a key role in the achievement of your clarity.

The ego plays back what we've learned, thus enhancing our confidence levels. When we get into spring cleaning, we gain a clear slate. The higher power within is the actuality of the ego. Clarity is an important aspect that goes with direction and decision in our lives. If your mind is not clear, your decisions are not free. Being prepared in life allows for more freedom.

Sometimes, when we find ourselves in too much space, and/or too much restricted space, we find ourselves on the edge of losing direction and focus. People allow hate to grow deep within themselves when they can't be clear about their decisions. When you move between the big and small, the superior and inferior, you allow an evolution to build from that space within. By evolving into the space in an expansive way, you allow a sense of freedom to give you a clear slate.

Clarity is about having and understanding the space in the body between the spine, the ribs, muscles, and tissues. It's articulation. It's also about freeing oneself from impurities. By having clarity, you have the spiritual space that takes over the body. This creates a definitive direction that leads us to our own path. By moving in between the light and dark, we find the way out of confusion. That's the purpose of clarity; to get out of your objective way.

Too much clarity, or not enough, creates a loss of direction and focus in life. In order to evolve into this clear space in an expansive way, allows for a sense of freedom.

Sometimes, when we find ourselves in isolation or alienation, we tend to become limited, moving out of that space, becomes a decision. By directing the body and using different parts, we gain the clarity that we need to move on. In order to be clear, we must first begin in purity. It is crucial to have a pure mind. We gain purity by releasing negativity. Purity begins in the heart—the support of the human race—the diet and life activity. In order to begin a life of purity, we must clear the mind of unnecessary thoughts and desires. The soul must be pure so the heart can sing.

Opening Your Heart to Your Feelings

The eyes are the opening we use to bond with the soul. They are the part of the body from which the 'gaze' from the depths of our hearts and souls begin to form. A person's soul shines forth from the eyes like a candle in a window on a dark night. Eye 'gazing' is the beginning of the deepest connection two people can ever make—even more than with intercourse. Astonishing, I know. During the next set of exercises, it is best to follow each motion with your eyes and also do the rapid eye movements. This helps the nervous system break patterns that may have been unhealthy. The eyes need to move to have strength and flexibility just like the rest of your body.

The eye segment is the one exercise you truly need to do since it opens the eyes, removing the armor and shields. This causes freedom in order for you to see clearly the plain truth. Practice looking into the eyes of others during the day. Practice blinking your eyes rapidly. Blinking keeps the eyes moist. Eye contact helps us connect with other people. Eventually, you will be so "free" that nothing can or will get in your way. Also, the ocular area needs rapid eye movement exercises for the purpose of expression. The eyes work with the rest of the body whether they are opened or closed.

When we make eye contact with another, it helps us let go of defenses, isolation and unnecessary boundaries. It breaks the fear of the unknown and prepares us to support our emotions better. Our emotions, when seen in the eyes, are revealed by the way we use the eye muscles. The eyes are the primal-movement, which is used during the interrelations we first encounter in the world. When our eyes open at birth, it is like waking up to the sunlight after a long night of sleep. Imagine being in a jail cell, in the dark for a month, then, coming out to face people. It is the eyes that tell us so much about a person, as if they are the pages in an open book. To maintain a romance, eye gazing is a good practice that will keep you connected spiritually and emotionally. Your eyes are an intimate part of your emotional space and need to be exercised by looking into the eyes of another. This is the way of our spirits.

Eye Gazing

Eye or soul gazing is an integral way of bonding. As you look into the eyes, when listening to your partner, friends, child, or whomever, you discover the way to the truth, authenticity, greater love, trust and, more importantly, making a connection. It's this connection that allows us entry to the other place, residing deep within us, known as the soul. We feed off each other's energy, thus, we feed our souls. In order to meet someone, your eyes must be unshielded, meaning you must remove your mask. It is this practice of looking into the eyes that makes you attractive to another human being and shows them you have a healthy level of self-confidence.

Unfortunately, a lot of people are armored and shielded with their eyes; therefore, they do not fully connect their entire self with another person. When we open to love, the defenses around the eye muscles unfold, and not only do we see more clearly, but people see us differently and our eyes become a welcoming light. Coming out through the eyes, opens the presence of your soul, allowing you to live a fuller life. To look deeply from the source within, into your own eyes, challenges your ability to see within yourself, bringing those gifts you possess forth through your eyes.

"Cry if you must to cleanse your eyes, for they are the windows to your soul." - Anonymous

- PRACTICE -

1)   RHYTHM & REPETITION: Partner necessary. One person is the listener while the other is the talker. The talker states his/her desires, boundaries and fears. Repeat this for 20 minutes and pay attention where it takes you verbally. The listener is to show no response, just to listen with respect and compassion and hold space. By being open and maintaining his/ her space, the listener develops good communication. Another exercise to try is, tell this person all the things you love about yourself. The listener just be present.

2)   HEAR WITH CLARITY: Partner necessary. The following are some questions to ask each other, taking turns. "What is it that you need from me?" "What can I do to make things feel clearer?" and, "Where are you right now in your life?"

3)   DIVINE COMMUNION: Partner necessary. One plays the talker, the other, the listener. Talker tells partner how he/she can have more passion, intimacy and enlightenment in his/her life. Go on claiming what it is that you need in your life for 10 minutes. The listener does not respond, hearing clearly with his/her heart.

4)   OPEN THE SPACE: No partner needed. Start clarity by freeing the body spaces. Begin by eating pure foods. Practice a kriya, such as colonics, fasting or nasal cleansing with a neti tea pot. Let go of one negative thought each week.

5)   VISUALIZE: No partner needed. While relaxed, close your eyes and visualize what it is that you need to do to make your life work better. While in this moment, see yourself following through with what you visualized.

6)   BRAG: Partner necessary. One person talks, your partner listens. Talker, clarify for your partner 3 positive things about you. Take it farther

by bragging to your partner about how amazing you are. Then brag about your body what you like and dislike.

7)   BONDING: Partner necessary. Sit comfortably, facing your partner. Begin gazing into each other's eyes for at least a full 5 minutes. One way to do this is, with both eyes, look into your partner's left eye. This is a form of kriya, which means to purify. By staring at your partner in this way, you are cleansing your soul, emptying your cup, purifying the moment, thus, bonding from a deep place. As you continue to gaze at one another, begin light communication. Tell your partner what you appreciate about them. Give them a wonderful compliment.

8)   FOCUS: Partner necessary. Sitting across from your partner, focus on each other's eyes. Then, take a full minute to tell this person what you love about yourself and vice versa. Next, tell this person what you want for yourself and your relationship. Then, tell your partner what you are feeling, emotionally, in your body.

9)   EYE GAZING: Sit in a semi dark room with a lit candle facing you. Begin to stare at this candle for 10 minutes while breathing in your nose and out your mouth. Sit in silence. Do once a week.

10)   SEE FROM THE HEART: No partner needed. Start today by looking in the eyes of those with whom you come in contact. It doesn't matter who it is, but make a solid connection. Look at them with your eyes and see them from your whole being, your heart. This is a wonderful practice to continue throughout the day and can lead to finding lasting friendships with those you solidly connect to. As a result, this practice will enhance your present relationship and open at deeper levels of appreciation.

CHAPTER 12

Kinepathics Approach
The Acknowledged Self

Liberation

Liberation means being free from a controlling influence in your life. It can be anything from a favorite food to a relationship that has grown luke-warm, yet comfortable, when you long for passion. Liberation is letting go of the thoughts and actions in which others have the control within your mind. It is the freedom to be you.

In order to truly be able to liberate, you must no longer have any doubts about yourself. Through willpower and discipline you will have gained control over your thoughts, emotions and actions. Your defenses and boundaries will be such that they are protective without cutting off your ability to attract others. The love inside you will have surfaced from its prison of baggage and emotional insecurity.

Liberation is about freeing your emotions, opening space in order that you may love yourself. It is about being able to breathe freely and expansively, which increases your sexual excitement and prolongs the wonderful feelings that go with it. Liberation is about being spontaneous, letting go of restrictions that keep you from being in the truth of the moment, so that you can be free to do what is important to you, whenever you need to. By breathing freely and properly, you are able to liberate yourself from anxiety and stress, while opening yourself to love and attention, inviting others in so they may know and love you.

Liberation is about facing and getting over your fears by allowing touch and being able to touch others. It is about attaining chi, or sexual energy. Liberation is about fluidity and the ability to feel comfortable in your own body. It is about healing yourself and opening your soul to the universe by communing with the higher being inside you. Liberation is about having achieved an innate strength and being confident about yourself—being comfortable with the "real you."It's opening up to your wildness.

Liberation is about having good communication skills and not being afraid to use them. When you are able to communicate with another person, you have made a solid connection—one that expresses your confidence. Liberation is about having clarity of the mind, body and soul. It is about having stability, balance and power within. It is being able to look into another's eyes, making a solid, lasting connection that opens up the possibilities for new relationships. When we attain the courage to walk away from a situation, a marriage, a job to save you; this is liberation

Finally, liberation is the ability to trust completely. It is the ability to leave all that is worldly as exactly as it is. It is about being able to move beyond the restrictions of our human forms and become the spiritual beings we are meant to be. Spiritualism is the final rung on the ladder of liberation. It is being able to freely reach out to another with trust, love and the complete awareness of who you are and who that other person is too. It is having the intuition to know what others around you need and the ability to teach them. When you have reached this level of liberation, you have attained the truest freedom of all.

"Only you can set yourself free." –Anita

- NOTES -

Sexuality / Spirituality / Sensuality

Spirituality is true freedom. It started out and usually stays centralized in the floor of the pelvis. We tend to open up and close down our spirits, only letting it out when we feel it's safe. However, the spirit is much stronger than we believe, so you should let it out and honor it for the precious unique gift it is. When we hide our spirit, we run from our soul. You need to step out of your human confines and let your spirit have the life it calls for. Spirits are attracted to other spirits so don't be afraid to let your spirit intertwine with another and feel the nourishment it both gives and receives. Spiritualism is the true religion of individual freedom. It is the freedom to be unique and expressive, to be who you are. Spiritualism is a liberation, the liberation of your heart—a wholesome, cleansing event and the integration of your soul. The only deity to look to is the Divine being within. Spirituality is about not being afraid to be who you are. That awareness and flexibility enables you to go and live a life that is free from boundaries and fears, truly trusting the self. When we have come this far, we have attained a perfect intimacy with the self, in that we are able to move within that freedom, reaching out toward another.

Spirituality, in its truest sense, involves the use of a flexible mind and a playful, free spontaneous nature. It's being the "real" you and finding your own truth. When you achieve this, you will have a "free spirit."

In order to achieve this paradise of the self, you must open your energy, coming into the feeling; to be able to give and receive. A person finds the highest level of freedom while making love, but only if they allow themselves to fully enjoy the experience—no inhibitions. You truly need to cultivate the freedom before you can go on to the level of the "free spirit." The freedom of life draws upon the incredible energy of your sexual self. This is the passion of who you are. Our energy, passion and fluidity flow from the entire body, beginning at the center of the pelvic cradle. Your body needs the sexual energy to move through it in order for you to be integrated, thus experiencing true freedom and the truth within you.

When we take advantage of others in a sexual way, we are taking away their freedom as well as our own. To reach the highest level of sensation causes the liberation of the feelings you experience with that other person, as well as the world all in one moment. The release spreads the energy—meaning that the liberation between the two of you will carry on. During the sexual revolution, people went out and expressed their physical freedom, but they neglected to develop their emotional, inner sensations, which led to mental armoring and conflict.

The key to avoiding this mental armoring and conflict is to constantly flush the emotions, always expressing by letting all the negativity out, screaming at the top of your lungs if you have to in order to get it all out, from the very beginnings from which we came—the womb, which is located in the pelvic cradle, where all energy sits.

Sex was once the darkness and is now seen as the creator and the seat of creativeness. In a sense, sexuality and spiritualism are one in the same and are to be dispersed, through one's own discipline, evenly among human-ness. At one time, religious institutions gave us the foundational security to spread out, be closer to one another; be comfortable with everyone—no racism. Instead, people use religion as a way of getting back to segregating again—by separating from those different. This is supposed to help us unionize from our soul and express the Godly freedom of our lives. It just so happens that the core of all religions is the same, just as the core of the human body and soul is the same. You must believe in yourself before any religion. Religion is a shell where many people go to hide and it keeps personalities inhibited by strict rules. People, as a general rule, are really all the same. This is a dilemma because most people truly hate themselves and don't want to identify through others. It is essential that they like themselves before they can like others. While not an old concept, it challenges the boundaries of conventional thinking.

What we strive for is the ability to connect the emotional, spiritual and sexual being into one being and have the ability to pay attention to the work it takes to connect them. Your spiritual self is but a degree of your truth—the "real you." Individual freedom is sparked by the true religion; that being Spiritualism. You must have control over your freedom in order to connect to your spiritual self.

The higher spirit begins with spirituality. There are no Gods to seek out, only the God within; the divine being inside you. Religion gives us a direction that will allow us to connect to our higher self. It directs us there instead of toward conflict and politics, which is sad since people make religion so political. This is why freedom begins in the body, the primal, the ritual being. Spiritualism is nothing more than the freedom that exists when we completely let go, living that wild inner being that screams to be free. Freedom is risky, but worth it to gain the great energy of the senses that ignites the passion for life and happiness.

The more we love ourselves, the farther we go to surrendering to our spirit. True fulfillment is to practice making love to all that you do in every moment. We all need to keep the love open or emptiness will surface. We need to stay in touch with the divine nature of our being.

Make Love to All That You Do

Love as an emotion, is terribly abused in the society of today. By making love to everything, we are giving of ourselves. When we learn to feel our senses and look at everything from a positive angle, we will be spreading more love than ever. Love is a powerful feeling and yet it remains invisible. Why? Because people are conditioned to hate, but underneath this deep hate is love. It is a very thin line. In order to experience love, we must allow ourselves to become vulnerable. Love as an emotion comes easy, yet it is so difficult for us to confront—to be a part of. Why? It's because, people push love away. With all the differences among people, think how love could make for a greater connection. The more you love, the more you liberate that love in others and the happier you will become.

The core of our happiness resides in the pelvic floor, meaning we must delve deep into that region, draw on that happiness and spread it out into our society. Love for some is a fearful emotion, especially if the love they received growing up was insufficient. Let go of the fear, because love conquers all. People have and still kill and die for love. It is the truest treasure we possess in that love is a combination of all the senses, the body, the mind and the sexual self all in one character. Love is a full integration of prosperity. It teaches us how to attend to our natural self; letting go of pretentiousness and becoming one with the world.

We are only people, but we treat ourselves as objects. The natural flow of love is within us all and it begins with honesty and respect for the self and others. There is no such thing as selfishness, but selflessness. Humanity wallows in a state of abuse, when the idea is to be in a happy state of mind, no matter what life hands us. Love allows us to let go of self judgment, the judgment of others and teaches us to respect all animals of nature, for this is from where the human in us derives. Allow yourself to come from a place of love. I know it can be challenging, especially if you haven't had much experience in that arena. Now is the time to begin something new for you. I promise that when you start to love, you will experience life to its fullest potential. It begins by forgiving yourself, your parents and all the people along the way that hurt you. Forgiveness is the withdrawal of judgment—the deliberate release of conflict, conviction, and non-acceptance. This is where love begins. Quit holding others responsible for your insufficiencies, imagined or otherwise. Quit blaming others. The heart muscle atrophies if love is not experienced.

Teach everyone around you how to love by demonstrating it in every conceivable way. The need to embrace and be embraced as well as knowing the true value of life is where love begins. Love is the highest healing power of all. The love of life can transform all of you like it did me when I was a child, suffering horribly with Rheumatic Fever, surrounded by hate. Each of us suffers something equally as horrible but every one of you can heal yourselves with that powerful love. Love has no limit or definition.

Freedom Within Structure

This kind of freedom is all about letting your hair down while keeping your focus. With a little liberated thinking, you can still feel free, even when you are in a committed relationship. You may wonder why people feel that being in a committed relationship means losing their freedom. It is because they don't understand that freedom is within, meaning it's the way they think—the way they feel in their own bodies. Whether or not you're in a relationship, you are not free if you're not open. Since freedom begins with self love, the relationship to the self helps to promote this freedom. The goal is to know the identity of the self so that you can release it and be boundless. How much freedom you attain is measured by how far you take it. Allow yourself the permission to be liberated in your thoughts. Let go of your inhibitions and open up your mind. Allow your soul to run wild. Take the veil from your mind so that you are free to new and different ideas. With just a little bit of focus, your committed relationships can be free and you can retain freedom in them.

Create the Change

Focus, boredom and ambition support change. Profound things happen when we make positive changes. Focus is your own responsibility, values and demands. Focus means being who you are and not taking on an identity that does not belong to you. Focus is a point, a place to move from, a place to be—a place to go. When you have focus, you also possess the core energy that is needed for you to shift. Perfect focus breaks the dimensions where stillness lives in the soul. When you are able to focus, you have come to the realization of the wonderful person you are and can face your aloneness with contentment.

Boredom is, in all actuality, peace. It leaves room for new horizons. Boredom is the state of readiness for something more, something better. When we are bored, it's not that we are tired of where we are, rather, we are growing and this is lag time. Boredom is not to be looked on unkindly, but welcomed and respected. When we feel bored, we need to come back to the part of the self that is stable and re-think how we feel. At times, boredom means a sense of unfinished business. If this is the case, take the time to examine it. . When things are taken from us this means that some-thing better is on the horizon.

To become ambitious is to be inspired by life and by your own passion. It is the true empathetic self that connects us to ourselves and others. To diversify is part of ambitious behavior. Ambition turns to self motivation. It says; "I like who I am, I like the universe, and I like my ability to connect in this way." Meditation en-lightens ambitious needs. Change is healthy. After it is all said and done, change still remains. It helps re-pattern the nervous system. When we don't change, we get stuck in patterns of fear, depression and the inability to create.

- PRACTICE -

1)   WILDDANCE™: No partner needed. Put on some music and begin dancing wildly around your home. Dance as if no one is watching. Dance like there's no tomorrow. Then begin to take off your clothes and dance around the house naked. Reflect on how it feels to be free. Experi-ence the moments of birth.

2)   CARESS: Partner necessary. Sit comfortably across from your partner, hold hands and stare into this person's eyes for 10 minutes. Have your partner close their eyes. You take one of their hands and guide it to your face. Have them gently explore your face blindly.   Then open the eyes and switch.

3)   LOVE BREATH: No partner needed. While standing in the mo-ment, begin to breathe in through your nose with your tongue on the roof of your mouth. Let your breath out the mouth with your teeth together, your lips spread in a smile. As you do this, focus on opening the heart and then feel it opening. Open the love with the breath flowing throughout your body, each and every cell, bone, muscle and tissue. Let your heart down by undoing the layers and feeling the pain that, essentially, is your pleasure. Do this for 20 minutes each day.

4)   LEG VIBRATION: Partner necessary. Begin by lying flat on

your back with your legs in the air. Breathe in and out through the mouth deeply, adding vibration to the legs. Keep shaking and vibrating the legs for at least 10 minutes. Remain in the present. Do this alone and then have your partner witness you do this and place their hand on our pelvis while making eye contact.

5)   LET GO: No partner needed. Reflect on both a small and a large occurrence of fear. Both are connected. By focusing on the small fear, you will help to reduce the larger fear. Once you let go of the smaller fear, you can begin to focus on the next fear that hinders you. Working in the spirit of your mind, write down all your fears, so you know which to work on next.

6)   NECK OPENING: Partner necessary. Sit behind your partner in a comfortable cross legged position. Allow yourself to surrender to your partner by dropping your neck in their hands. The partner is to follow the direction of your neck movement and encourage more movement of your neck.

7)   CHAKRA NOURISH: Partner necessary. Lie flat on your stomach. Your partner is to place his/her hands along the spine from the tail bone upward, sweeping the energy upward then, pat the spine gently.

8)   BACK TO BACK: Partner necessary. Sit on the floor back to back with your arms interlaced. Feel the point of contact as you both rock gently back and forth. Increase the movements in, out and around while staying connected to your partner's back.

9)   JOURNAL: No partner needed. Describe a negative experience in your life. Then describe a positive experience you had in your life. Write a page about both.

10)   JOURNAL 2: No partner needed. Write a negative experience about your pelvis and a positive one. Open a relationship with your pelvic core. What might you be afraid to receive sexually? What are you afraid to give sexually? What do you get sexually that you don't want? What do you give sexually that you want?

11)   THE SCREAM: No partner needed. Walk around your open

space and scream. Scream at the top of your lungs. Stop and take in 5 breaths, holding your head as if you're pulling your hair and begin to scream again. Make a statement such as: "I am so angry!" or "I am pissed off!" Just continue letting it all hang out. Best to go to an ocean or the mountains.

12)   CHAOTIC MOMENT: No partner needed. Place on a table items such as pots and pans. Begin circling the table, rearranging the items, making noise with them by clashing the pans together. Move them from one table to another. Do this for approximately 10 minutes at a fast pace then a slow pace. Feel the incremental moments within the space, connect to the sound.

"Allow your inner child to come out and play. By so doing, you are allowing the liberation of the love within you. Throw your head back, laugh. Let go and live free." – Anita

GLOSSARY

Abandonment: This is a feeling of desertion. It is when someone walks out on you where there was a responsibility. It is about the loss of love itself, the crucial loss of connectedness. It involves breakup, betrayal and aloneness. It is a feeling of isolation in a relationship; it stems back to childhood. It's when a pet dies, or a parent leaves a child, even when you're feeling unaccepted by a group of your peers.

Ajna Chakra: Energy center located behind the forehead, also called psychic centre-one of the seven energy centers. It is situated between the eyebrows. Otherwise known as the third eye.

Akashic Records: A Sanskrit term used to describe a compendium of mystical knowledge encoded in a non-physical plane of existence. It is the knowledge of experience.

Anger: An emotional state that may range from minor irritation to intense rage. Anger is an emotion necessary for grounding and survival. It is the emotion that if not exercised suppresses pleasure and happiness.

Asana: This is a yoga posture or poses called yogasana. A balanced position for smooth energy flow in specific areas of the body and mind. In yoga, Sanskrit is used for the names of the different poses or asanas.

Ashtanga: Ashtanga yoga is the system of yoga taught by Sri K. Pattabhi Jois at the Ashtanga Yoga Research Institute in Mysore, India. This yoga involves synchronizing the breath with a progressive series of postures.

Ashwini Mudra: The practice of contracting the anal sphincter located in the perineum.

Aura: An energy field that surrounds in and around the physical body.

Bhagavad Gita: An episode in India's great epic, the Mahabharata. It is a war between two branches of the Kaurava family. The Gita is a conversation between Krishna and Arjuna.

Bandhas: Are muscular locks that seal in the energy. Moola Bandha located is the energy lock created by the contraction of the perineum in the male and the cervix in the female.

Bardo: The transcendence between death and rebirth.

Bioenergetics: A therapy invented by Dr. Alexander Lowen. Body stress exercises that compliment Dr. Wilhelm Reich's work in reducing body armor.

Bodhicitta: In Buddhism it is the road to enlightenment; a freeing of the suffering that keeps us trapped in cyclic experiences (samsara). To achieve this one must learn wisdom and compassion for all things.

Bonding: Part of bonding is when we develop an intimate personal connection with another human being. Maternal bonding begins with eye contact between a mother and new born.

Chakras: A chakra is a center of activity that receives, assimilates, and expresses life force energy. It means wheel. There are seven chakras that align along the subtle body. Chakras are psychic centers used for spiritual concentration. On a physical level, chakras are associated with the major nerve plexus and endocrine glands in the body.

CHH: Stands for Childrens Heart Hospital located in Pennsylvania. The far away hospital where I spent six long months.

Chi: Chi energy is a word from the Chinese. It means the fluid flow of energy that stimulates the meridians and opens the connective tissue.

Connective Fascia Tissue: Fascia is the soft tissue component of the connective tissue system that permeates the human body. It surrounds the muscles, bones, organs, nerves and blood vessels. Fascia functions as the body's first line of defense against infections. After injury it is the fascia that creates an environment for tissue repair.

Cremation: Cremation is the act of reducing a corpse to ashes by fire of extreme heat within a crematorium furnace.

Dance Movement Therapy: The therapeutic use of body movement to improve the mental and physical well-being of a person. It focuses on the connection between the conscious and subconscious being in order to promote health and healing.

Denial: One is in denial when they don't accept what is going on in their lives or what was in their past. It is a defense mechanism whereby a person is faced with a fact and is too uncomfortable to accept it, so they reject it instead of insisting that it isn't true in spite of what may be overwhelming evidence.

Dharma: The teachings of the Buddha which lead to the enlightenment path of awakening into one's life purpose.

Divine Mother: The God in the feminine, the Goddess. The divine mother abides in the heart of every human being. Any mother Goddess, a concept of Hinduism.

Empathy: Having the awareness to recognize or understand another person's state of mind or emotion. It is often characterized as the ability to put oneself in another's shoes or experience another's emotions.

Faith: Having belief, being positive. Having hope.

G-Spot: Also known as the sacred spot or Grafenberg-spot or Goddess spot. It is located behind the front wall of the yoni or vagina, behind the public bone toward the belly. Stimulation creates expansion of the tissue and heals the hidden pain of trauma.

Gesture: The physical expression of the hands or body we engage to make a point or reference, sometimes pointing the finger is negative or embracing.

Hatha: Ha means sun and tha is the moon. All yoga is based on the hatha foundation of breathing and postures that balances the yin/yang energies.

Higher Power: A power greater than ourselves-when humans became conscious of the self it is a force that was better than the ego mind.

Hinduism: This is an Indian religious tradition, often referred to as Sanatana Dharma. It means eternal law.

Holding Space: To be present with your full self to another human being. To be physically, emotionally, spiritually and mentally available for another's moments in process. To let go of judgmental thinking and be open to listening.

Ida Nadi: Moon nadi corresponding to the parasympathetic nervous system.

Jivanmukta: Jivan means one who lives; mukta means liberated. A liberated living being or realized saint. A jivanmukta is involved in the world for the sake of humanity without personal attachment. Even though they appear normal, the seeds of all mental impressions are completely burnt out; they are essentially living the truth.

Kama Sutra: The classical Indian treatise on the foundation of love. Written by Vatsyayana. It means to weave together the art of love.

Karma: Action and reaction. The present, past and future experiences thus making one responsible for ones own life and the pain and joy it brings to him/her.

Kundalini: A psycho-spiritual energy, the energy of the consciousness, which is thought to reside within the sleeping body and is aroused either through spiritual discipline or spontaneously to bring new states of consciousness. Kundalini is Sanskrit for snake or serpent power which sits at the root chakra at the base of the spine. The power of Kundalini is said to be enormous. Those having experienced it, claim it to be indescribable. Kundalini is accessed through breath, yoga and meditation. It is said that Kundalini opens new pathways in the nervous system.

Liberation: This is when we let go of the thoughts that control our mind. When we give ourselves the permission to love again and when we stop caring what people think; just being who you are. It takes courage to liberate in a society that is governed. It is spiritual freedom.

Lingam: Sanskrit for the male sexual organ (penis). It is the wand of Shiva.

Love: Love is the feeling of bliss. It represents a range of human emotions and experiences related to the senses of affection and sexual attraction. Love is a powerful emotion that can be overwhelming and intimidating. To love another we must learn to love ourselves first.

Mantra: Subtle sound vibration. A group of words or word that are repetitively recited to expand consciousness.

Meridian: Traditional Chinese medicine known as a channel. They are stimulated during acupuncture and acupressure treatments.

Mudra: Hand gestures or attitudes, it is a Sanskrit word. Mudras can be described as psychic, emotional, devotional and aesthetic gestures of attitudes. Mudra is introduced after one has attained pranayama and asana.

Nadis: The passageway for the flow of energy in the psychic body. There are 72,000 of them.

Nirvana: The Buddha described nirvana as the perfect peace of the mind that is free from craving, anger and other affiliate states. Liberation follows nirvana. Nirvana is the highest happiness.

Paglia, Camille: An American author, teacher, social critic and dissident feminist. Author of *Sexual Personae* and many more; professor at University of the Arts in Phila.

Pantanjali: Compiled the Yoga Sutras of knowledge. These are a collection of aphorisms on yoga and life philosophy. He codified the eight fold path that teaches non-stealing, non-violence and austerity.

Patience: A state of endurance under difficult circumstances. Being patient helps us learn more about who we are. Taking time for you is patience. Having awareness is patience.

Perineum: It is the area of the lower pelvic floor in males and females between the symphysis pubis and the coccyx. It includes the anus in males and vagina in females.

Pingala: Sun nadi; corresponding to sympathetic nervous system.

Polyamory: It is the practice of having more than one intimate relationship with the consent of all involved.

Pranayama: This is the life force within the body. Prana means life force and yama means to extend. The more life force we have, the longer our lives are.

Presence: Means being aware and in the moment. The sacred force of Shakti brings on more presence in the personality. When the Kundalini is open, one is said to be present. Being present is being alive and dynamic.

Psoas Muscle: The muscles that lie along the lumbar region of the spine. It is part of the hip flexor group. Releasing this muscle through movement and massage keeps the structural ability strong.

Pubococcygeal Muscles: PC muscle is a hammock like muscle, found in both sexes that stretch from the pubic bone to the coccyx forming the floor of the pelvic cavity and supporting the pelvic organs.

Puja: This is a Hinduism tradition which means ritual, worship or offering. This is a sacred place that is manifested as an altar at home, a temple or a special place of worship. In tantra workshops it is called a chakra puja where we awaken the senses and honor the divinity in each being..

Rebirthing-Breathwork: A form of alternative medicine consisting of a breathing technique. Leonard Orr developed this method because he believed that human birth was traumatic. The breathing helps to relieve past memories of the birth that live within the cells.

Reich,Wilhelm M.D.: Dr Wilhelm Reich invented the orgone energy breath, he believed that dysfunctional breathing patterns as a child contribute to behavioral dysfunction as an adult. Within the muscle character sits armor, the unexpressed emotions that need release.

Rheumatic Fever: An inflammatory disease that develops after streptococcal throat infection. This disease is responsible for many damaged heart valves.

Rhythm: Rhythm is any measured flow of movement. It is connecting the beat to the heart. Rhythm is the time within a beat.

Samadhi: is a Hindu and Buddhist term which means higher levels of concentrated meditation or dhyana. It is the eight and final limb of the Yoga Sutras. One experiences Samadhi when the mind becomes still or concentrated although the person remains conscious. A state of complete control over the distractions of consciousness. Being aware of one's existence without thinking. Being detached from the intellect.

Samskara: In Buddhism it is referred to the cycle of birth and death and can only be escaped through enlightenment. It is the suffering that comes from ignorance. Ones karmic "account balance" at the time of death is inherited via the state at which a person is reborn. If one lives in evil ways they are reborn as an animal or other unfortunate being.

Sanskrit: This is a classical language of India and a liturgical language of Hinduism.

Shakti: Meaning sacred force, power or energy, it is the Hindu concept or personification of the divine feminine aspect, which is sometimes referred to as "The Divine Mother." Shakti represents the active, dynamic principles of feminine power.

Shaktipat: The act of a guru or spiritual teacher conferring a form of spiritual power of awakening on a student. Shaktipat can be administered through word, thought or touch.

Shiva: Shiva is the male force in action, the destroyer of the world. Shiva is the god of the yogis, both celibate while at the same time, a lover of his spouse. Shiva is one of the principle deities of Hinduism.

Tantra: The practice of tantra shows us how to reclaim the sexual intimacy that is our birthright. It promotes love, and sacred sexuality. Tantra emerged in India more than 6000 years ago; it started as a rebellion against organized religion, which held that sexuality should be rejected in order to reach enlightenment. Tantra means to manifest, to weave, to expand consciousness and to weave together the polarities of the male and female into the harmonious whole.

Undulation: The wave within the experience of the somatic body. All the fluids of the body function as one undulating stream of intelligence. A wavelike motion to and from in a fluid or elastic medium propagated continuously among its particles. The pulsation caused by the vibrating together of two tones not quite in unison. It is the wave motion that softens our defenses and allows the life of the body to be in action. Undulation brings life to the body as a whole. The fluid system has to keep transforming itself. It is the youth in action.

Vatsyayana: He is the author of the Kama Sutra. The Kama Sutra is a Sanskrit book about love.

Yab Yum: A traditional Tibetan Buddhist (literally father-mother) image of two deities sitting in a sexual meditation position to help one achieve the insight that leads to spiritual liberation.

Yin/Yang: In the Taoist it is the relationship of the masculine and feminine energies coming together in the path of union to form a collective energy of love. One is the opposite of the other.

Yoga: An Indian spiritual path aimed at achieving the union with the supreme consciousness. It is a practice of asana as a form of exercise. Yoga is a union occurring between the mind, body, spirit and breath.

Yoni: The feminine energy of source (vagina). The sacred temple or holy home of divinity.

Most Influential People in my Life

It is difficult when you look back over a lifetime and try to remember all the people whose path you crossed and vice versa. So many of them, some long term, others but a brief encounter, and yet all of them touch our lives and end up having a direct bearing on some of the decisions we make. This page is dedicated to those wonderful souls who influenced my life the most and encouraged me toward my path of enlightenment.

The first, and no doubt the person who had the most influence in my life was my mother. I celebrate the life she has given me. I learned from the many falls she took, not only in our family life, but from her life in general. It was the traumas she suffered that taught me a great deal about pain, sorrow and mistrust. I not only lived and experienced those moments but, I observed them daily.

There were teachers that were instrumental in guiding me along my path as I grew to adulthood, one of the most prominent being my 9th grade algebra teacher, Mrs. Grubbs. I learned a great deal about love and connection from the relationship I considered to be more than your average teacher/student association. It was of a spiritual connection.

As an adult, I had the honor to meet and be encouraged by spiritual leader Marianne Williamson and relationships guru, Sondra Ray. After I moved to California, I was further influenced by Marianne Karou, Bond Wright, Gabrielle Roth, Michelle Boston, Emily Conrad, Gurmukh, Ana Halprin, Ana Forest, Simone Forti, Margo Anand, Saraswati, Manuso Manos, Steve and Lokita Carter, Charles and Caroline Muir and so many more. My friend Francois Favre has influenced me greatly who is living in the Philipppines presently.

Of course there were many more and I am taking this opportunity to thank all of them from the deepest core of myself, the heart. I look forward to all those precious souls I still have to meet and the lessons we can both teach and learn from each other.

About the Author

At the age of nine in 1966, Anita was hospitalized for six months with rheumatic heart disease. It was at this time in her life that she cultivated wisdom. Being alone and away from home, confined to a bed without privileges, helped her to open up to her feelings and cultivate the relationship to the self. Being the only white child among African-American children in the hospital taught her that love goes beyond race and this was a transformative moment for her that people are just coming to embrace today. She felt so connected to the medical field from that young age that she later trained and worked as an x-ray technologist for 15 years. She went on to receive bachelor and master of arts degrees in psychology/dance movement. A registered therapist, yoga and tantra educator, she is also a certified Reichian and Bioenergetics therapist. A two-time national award winning medical journalist, she writes a weekly column called Love Buzz for www.centurycitynews.com

Anita moved to Los Angeles and presently remains a resident of both California and Philadelphia, PA, her home state. She has collected many experiences and explored many different aspects of life. Gifted with intuitive brilliance and liberated thinking, she has the ability to bring out what is hidden within people. She has been told that she makes people feel like they can be themselves when in her presence. Anita is a natural healer who believes and lives her own truth, which is the power of love.

Epilogue

After spending 15 years in Los Angeles, I have recently moved back to the Philadelphia/New York area to embrace change as well as what is familiar. I am practicing being bi-coastal for now as I am a resident of both states and deciding where to land my wings next. I have so much freedom, I may just stay in flight. After doing many years of work on myself with Kinepathics, I can say that I live and reflect from my truth. I live in the present and make my decisions from the deep truth. The only thing left in this life is love, and if I can move some people into freeing this powerful emotion, the world will be an easier place to live. The next step to ending the suffering is accepting the modern world, engaging the "new way", no matter what stage of life we are in. We need to open up to the world and participate in the evolution of wholeness. Our impulses are the evolution of creative spirituality. Hopefully after reading this book that you will be able to find that connection of spirituality and enlightenment and what it means in todays world. All suffering is an opportunity to love, to grow and be inspired by love. It takes backbone to live your life as you truly see fit, to emerge from society's norms. It is the abusiveness that we live that keeps us discontented. It is the creative impulse that we learn to identify with, this force coming from the sexual source of unlimited knowledge that derives its power when connected to the universe. It is you and the world. Use your power to connect to the universe.

NOT QUITE THE END...

Teacher Training Programs & Workshops

The teacher training program is designed for those who want to learn the Kinepathics approach to physical, emotional and sexual wholeness. The program teaches the six approaches to life solutions and evolution. Scripts of Tantra Wisdom™ and Yoga Sutra are part of the path to enlightenment. One must also stay connected and be committed to the inner path of the self. For further information, visit **www.kinepathics.com** or contact Anita at **anita@kinepathics.com** , info@tantrawisdom.com